© 2017 Kashlee Kucheran

The High Maintenance Minimalist

All rights reserved. No portion of this book may be reproduced in any form without permission from the publisher, except as permitted by Canadian and U.S. copyright law.

For permissions contact:hello@thehighmaintenanceminimalist.com

Paperback ISBN: 9781973353850

This book is for information purposes only. Although the Author has made every effort to ensure that the information in this book was correct at the time of press, the Author does not assume and hereby disclaim any liability to any party for any loss, damage or disruption caused by this book. The Author and/or distributors are not responsible for any adverse effects resulting, directly or indirectly, from the use or the suggestions outlined in this book or worksheets. Neither the author nor the publisher is engaged in rendering legal, accounting, or other professional services by publishing this book. If any such assistance is required, the services of a qualified financial professional should be sought.

Visit www.traveloffpath.com

Cover by: Victoria Kenzington

How to Use This Book:

This book is designed to be read while using the companion WORKBOOKS.
I have made both printable and online editable workbooks you should access before you start reading.
Download them at traveloffpath.com/workbooks

I want you to do more than just READ this book. I want you to take action on the things that make a true impact on your life.
Print off the workbooks to use in tandem with reading, or save the editable files on a device where you can easily access them.

Introduction 5

PART ONE 10

TRAPPED 10
1 - Why is everything so HEAVY? 11
2 - The EFFECTS of STUFF 15
3 - The Template of Life 22
4 - Is Minimalism the Answer? 34
5 - The Turning Point 45

Part TWO 47

Mindset 47
6 - Know Your WHY 48
7 - Take Action 55
8 - Need vs Want 63

Part THREE 79

START 79
9 - Let's Make A Budget 80
10 - Get out of debt 85
11 - Let Go & Downsize 92
12 - Declutter & Sell Your Old Crap 99

PART FOUR 108

Plan and Save 108
Chapter 13 Saving & Investing 109
14 - When you actually need to spend 117
15 - Budget Hacks 128

Part Five 131

EARN 131
16 - That Entrepreneur Life 132
17 - Your Dream Job 140
18 - Building Your Own Empire 155

Part Six 165

TRAVEL 165
19 - Drool Worthy Bucket List 166

20 - FLY 173
21 - STAY 177
22- Travel like a PRO 187

Part Seven 203

Go ALL IN 203
23- The Pro's and Con's 207
24 -Become a Digital Nomad 220
25 - Going ALL IN...without leaving home 241

Part Eight 244

Families 244
26 - Doing all of this with KIDS 245
27 - Families who are doing it! 255

Part Nine 263

FREEDOM 263
Acknowledgements 273
Resources & Extras 274
About The Author 275

Introduction

Have you ever been totally and utterly overwhelmed with daily life? Only to hear someone say "Suck it up buttercup, that's just the way it is!"

Well I happen to disagree immensely.

I wanted you to know a little bit about me before we go on this wild journey together because we are going to talk about some pretty intimate things: our desires, fears, regrets, and deepest wishes.

In the spirit of full disclosure, I am not a financial expert, nor am I a psychologist. I don't have a PHD or a MBA, but I do have a ton of life experience that I want to share with you. I have perfected the art of high maintenance minimalism, essentially meaning; I do more with less like a boss. I'm not into the empty white washed room kind of minimalism. Instead I'm into being debt free, traveling the globe, all while still being a modern woman. (I still need my heels, okay!)

My life wasn't always this clear.
I've been there, through the ups and downs.
I've scraped by one year at $15,000 and I've thrived some years raking in over $200,000. I've worked the 9-5 grind and the self-employed route. I've been tied into rat race bondage and experienced the giddy sensation of freedom. I'm sharing my personal experience with you in the hope it will give you some answers to your own questions.

Recently my husband Trevor and I just said "F*CK IT!", sold our home, 95% of our belongings, all to travel the world for the next 10 years. If reading that just made your ears perk up, then this book is for you.
Why would we do such a wild, and crazy thing?
Because we were tired of living a life that we didn't choose and felt we had little control over.

I've always felt this strange feeling, sometimes deep in the pit of my stomach, that I wasn't doing what I was born to do and I wasn't living the way I wanted to live. People say that is a normal feeling and it's healthy to question our lives from time to time. This wasn't an occasional feeling. This was an every single day kind of feeling. But shhhhhh…. Don't talk about it too much, or the crabs in the bucket will feel compelled to pull you back into the herd.

I'm not okay with sitting back silent anymore.
Something is wrong with our world and what is considered 'normal'. There are times when I can't even fathom why this isn't being talked about daily! Money, and the compulsive spending of that money, has taken front stage leaving 'experiences' in the nose bleed section. We are stuck inside the oily cog of consumerism, for the sole purpose of spinning a wheel to nowhere.

To sum it up: **We're trapped doing shit we hate, surrounded by shit we haven't even paid for yet.**
In my humble human (in case you were wondering if I was a robot) opinion, LIFE is not meant to look like this.

When Trevor and I started sharing our story of leaving the mundane, materialistic world behind, people started listening. We soon found our inbox full to the brim with emails asking for help on everything from budgeting to decluttering to traveling more. People were sharing their stories of how debt was affecting their well-being; they felt like they weren't even living, or how they had lost all hope with the mess they had gotten themselves in. It turns out we were not the only people who felt the weight of society crushing down upon them.
I knew I had to do something.

"Write a book!" Trevor said.
In my experience, most self-help books out there containing any financial chapters were either a total snooze fest, or they were unforgivingly rigid. You could choose between Wall Street legalese or do nothing and pinch every penny.

Can't a girl get some real world advice??

Trevor was right, I had to create something that would be relevant to people in our fast moving, neon lit world. Something that would combine a conversation about debt and not feeling good enough, because aren't those two things delicately intertwined with one another?!

Over the past 10 years, I have been desperately looking for something to fill an empty spot in my soul. I started searching in all the wrong places, but eventually found the right path.
I've finally found what makes me happy and now I must scream it from the rooftops, for everyone to hear.

Balance. Living with less. Freedom.

Such simple concepts yet so elusive to many.
While there is no blueprint for a more simple way of life, inside this book I have tried to create a manual of sorts that you can follow to achieve your own version of bliss.

I'll get straight to the point. Here are some of the things covered inside these pages:

- ✓ Why you spend so much money
- ✓ How to dramatically cut down your monthly cost of living
- ✓ Making a budget that isn't a total buzz kill
- ✓ Tips on paying down debt fast and keeping it from coming back
- ✓ How to declutter and actually make killer dough on your old junk
- ✓ The actual harm spending is doing and the benefits of letting go
- ✓ Strategies for saving money that will have your bank account feeling abundant
- ✓ Minimalism tools for singles, couples and families
- ✓ How to create a secondary stream of income
- ✓ Creating a profitable brand, business or hobby
- ✓ How to travel more frequently and see more on your bucket list
- ✓ The inside scoop on how to go all in with full time travel

In a nut shell: **How to stop wasting time and money and start living a life by design.**

We were faced with a choice recently that changed our lives forever. We had almost $25,000 in credit card debt, a home (with a 6 figure mortgage owing) and bills that were piling up. It doesn't sound unmanageable, but it could have gotten a lot worse.
Traveling 4-6 months of the year, we were paying bills even when we weren't home. Pair that up with some bad spending habits and a lust for more travel and you can see how quickly this can turn into a slippery slope.
In fact, I had just gone down that dangerous path a few years prior. A path that led me into a full-fledged melt down and I wasn't about to repeat it.

We quickly realized we would rather be traveling and spending our money on experiences instead of 'things', so we took some major action on turning our finances around to allow WAY more freedom! That meant making some massive changes, both mentality and physically, like selling our home, most of our stuff and becoming nomadic.

Since becoming completely debt free we have made the transition into full time travel. Every few months we pick a different city/country to live and work in, which has been our dream all along. This nomadic, material free life is not for everyone. I'm not suggesting you follow our exact steps. Maybe you just want to be debt free, period. Or perhaps you want to be able to travel a few weeks more a year. Or upgrade the type of travel you are doing. Whatever your goals, this will help get you there. This book will cover everything I've personally done to crush debt and tackle my bucket list.

This is not a "quit your job and get rich" kind of book. *(Gag me)*
Unless you are a lottery winner or born with a silver spoon dangling from your mouth, you need to WORK in order to live. You also need to hustle to create any type of wealth.
A guide that claims you can quit your job and carelessly travel the globe while millions pour into your bank is 100% full of horse dung.

Instead, this book is going to teach you how to think for yourself, pick your own path in life, stop wasting money on junk you don't need and take more world adventures.

What if you hate your job? If your career looks more like 'Office Space' on repeat, and you have a skill and a passion for something else, I would highly suggest digging into the EARN chapter of this book. Many people want to keep their 9-5 and just learn to make the hours in between count for more. We'll cover that as well.

One last thing I want you to know before we dive in.
There are some sections of this book that might make you angry. You might even draft an email to me, pointing out everything you disagree with, just to hit delete before sending.
GOOD. That means you needed to hear it. Even if you don't agree with my opinions, any emotional reaction to my words means it struck a chord. You might not be ready to admit that, but sooner or later you will discover why it got you so hot under the collar and massive growth will follow.
Side note: if you do decide to send me that email; great! I'd love to chat!

PART ONE

TRAPPED

1 - Why is everything so HEAVY?

Look around. Do you see it?
Yes, all the things around you this very moment.
Really stop reading and look.
How many of these things do you regularly use? How many things did you honestly forget were even there? If your place was robbed right now and they only took what was in the drawers and under the stairs, how long would it take you to notice?

Now what about the things you own, but can't see right now.
The debts that need repaying. Like the balance on your credit card. Or the amount owing on your student loans. Or the Sephora shipment that is on its way to your doorstep right now, filled with new makeup that you likely already have. Maybe even the storage unit that's full of junk, or the garage stuffed with boxes. Oh god, how long is this list already!!!!

How about the things you don't yet own, but are taking up a lot of mental real estate. Can you picture what they look like? It might be that Chanel bag you've been obsessing over, really shouldn't buy, but probably are going to anyway. Or that cute house you imagine playing Susie Homemaker in, but haven't really realized is going to be $3000/m to maintain.

Do you feel light or heavy right now? **Chances are you feel as heavy as a lead weight.**

Whoever said life was meant to feel this dang HEAVY!?
It's like that statement on your credit card with a $10,000 limit says: "By paying the minimum balance, this will take you 47 years and 10 months to pay off". That's heavy shizz right there. In fact, that's a LIFETIME of heavy. It's not just weight on your wallet, but also of your mind, emotions and even your physical body.
I felt that same weight and pressure.

Which seems almost ridiculous to me in retrospect because it was ME who crafted and created that life revolving solely around things, stuff and 'more'. Nobody held a gun to my head, I did it willingly, all on my own.

It all began when my Real Estate career started taking off. After years of grinding and hard work, my phone was lighting up like Drake's hotline bling. I was making more money in a month than I used to make in an entire year.
Sounds great, right?
Well it was for a little while, *until I lost all control.*

I thought I was really cool.
So cool in fact, that I could stay out all night drinking myself into black-out oblivion and expect to have myself pulled together the next day.
Or have zero responsibilities in my relationship.
Oh, and I could just freely spend every cent I earned because I could always just make more.
I watched myself let credit card balances climb from 3 figures, to 4 figures, to a whopping 5 (the horror). I was conscious (some might argue brain dead) when I decided to buy 2 cars and build a 3000 sq ft house that I didn't need. There was no Jiminy Cricket on my shoulder the day I blew $7,000 in one pop at Burberry. I just did it, and to tell you the truth, it felt fun (at the time). It was a wild ride through every material desire I had ever fantasized about. A full cart binge-a-thon like a real life PacMan eating every consumable thing in sight, looking on fleek the whole time.
Adrenaline surging, ego pumping, YOLO yelling, tornado that could only be fueled by MORE.

Oh yeah,
And then came the part where I totally crashed and burned.

Why wasn't all this STUFF making me happy!? I thought money could buy happiness and the people who said otherwise were just poor and envious. By that poisoned reasoning, I should have been the happiest person in the world. But I wasn't and my weaknesses started seeping out of the cracks.

After I couldn't hide the lies, the white powdery substance in bathroom stalls and my 'holier than thou' attitude any longer, I hit rock bottom. Everything in my life, including my closest relationships, came tumbling down. I was crippled by the debt and the pressure to perform.
I lost my money, my then fiancé, many of my fair weathered friends and pulled the plug on my career.
My saving grace was that I also lost my 'more More MORE' mentality along with all the rubbish.

I had to learn how to walk again like a newborn fawn, clumsy and timid, but motivated to keep going. To relearn things you already know can sound like an embarrassment, but I'm now proud to have gone through my rock bottom and come out with some wisdom. Since my meltdown (and losing a $200k a year salary) I've been smacked in the face with where I went wrong and how to avoid it in the future.
'Out of sight, out of mind' is not one of those strategies.

If I had to pin point the reason I went through such a rollercoaster ride, it would come down to this:
I wasn't doing what truly made me happy.
I was doing what I thought SHOULD make me happy. And when that didn't work, I tried numbing the pain with instant gratification. When that didn't work, I tried self-medicating with drugs and alcohol. And when that didn't work, I lashed out at people because I was angry with myself. It was like groundhog day, except there was no Bill Murray.

I was living a life that was against everything I valued: time with friends and family, traveling the world, helping others, learning new skills and languages, experiencing culture. Those were the values that meant the most to me in the world.
Instead I was trading in time, love and experiences for cold hard cash. No wonder I couldn't keep that charade going any longer.

Living a life that is based around core values is the measure of true wealth.

Can money and happiness co-exist together? Absolutely they can. But happiness can't live in the dark shadow of debt, uncertainty, materialism and greed.

Knowledge is Power

Have you ever heard the story of the boiling frog? If you put a frog in an already boiling pot of water, it will jump straight out. BUT if you put that same frog in warm water and slowly heat the water up to boiling, the frog won't even notice how hot the water has gotten until it's boiled to death. Pretty dang dramatic, right?!
I was that frog. My bucket was a house and the water was 'things' I filled it with. The heat was the debt, spending habits and attitude that was slowing starting to burn me. The only difference between me and that frog was I knew damn well that water was too hot to handle.
Just like me and that poor little frog, how many of us let debt, materialism, bad spending habits, comparison and clutter quietly sneak into our lives until they consume everything?

The good news:
It doesn't have to get to the 'boiling' point for you to do something about it!
Together, you and I are going to tackle some of the biggest issues our society faces and then how to sashay right by them into the sunset.

First, we need to know what we're dealing with.
Knowledge is power!

2 - The EFFECTS of STUFF

Mental & Emotional

Everything in this universe has matter. It all has weight. Even thoughts! The 10 extra pairs of jeans in your dresser that you never wear are taking up a lot more than just physical drawer space.
The things in our lives can take up a lot of mental and emotional space as well.
We can feel guilty for never using the items, and double guilt for not doing anything about it. It can make us feel not good enough if they happen to be too small, (because NO woman has ever bought clothing that she will 'work to fit into') which sends us into a downward spiral of internal name calling (we are hardest on ourselves). Those jeans can even affect your future happiness, by stopping you from being able to afford to go on that Cabo getaway because those 10 pairs of jeans literally add up to $2100 spent.
This is just a small example of the actual weight the things we own have on our lives.

Debt, clutter and materialism can cause mental stress, anxiety, anger, guilt, shame, depression and a litany of other negative emotions. These feelings can put unnecessary strain on our relationships, jobs, and even the way we talk to ourselves.

So why do we put ourselves through this?

The Federal Reserve estimates that nearly half of Americans can't scrape together $400 in an emergency without borrowing or selling something.
Which makes me ask: Then WHY do we line up for the next iPhone or feel the need to have 3 flat screens in our homes, if we can barely survive until next month?

Comparison and Fast Fashion

Never before in history have we had such a window into each other's lives. Instagram stories, Facebook photos, status updates and live video allow us to watch and covet what each other have at all times of the day and night. Now that we are all being watched, we need to look our best! Have the newest things! Keep up appearances! Don't forget to smile!
What we don't see is how we are playing a very dangerous ego driven game with each other. A game that no one can actually win.

People are getting more and more depressed. Researchers have noticed a major upswing in mental health issues revolving around anxiety and depression in adults. What's really scary is this: Rates of depression and anxiety among teenagers have increased by 70 per cent in the past 25 years. How much of the increase in depression and anxiety has to do with comparison, debt, compulsive spending, being overworked, under paid and the pressures of social media?
If you find yourself the victim of a crime, you can go to the police to get help. But what if you become a victim to emotional, mental and even physical pain because of compulsive comparison? Who do you call? Sadly, Ghostbusters is not the answer. New research is suggesting that one of the main sources of our despair is comparing ourselves to others, and worse yet, spending money to try and be more like them.

The oh so wise philosopher Macklemore stated in his musical art piece Thirftshop, "I call that being tricked by business"
Dude is bang on.

Fast fashion is like that guy in your building who seduced you, only until he got what he wanted and then won't return your calls. So you make sure your hair is curled and your outfit is on point every time you check the mail, just in case you bump into him and you can show him what he's missing! They (fast fashion and the ass in your building) both used you and will likely use you again when they see how desperate you are.
I say quit pining for the latest trend at the mall and be classic! The only people who notice you are wearing the latest 'x', are others who have also been swindled into the fast fashion trap.

A big reason we just want to buy that super cute cable knit sweater and ankle booties is because we see it on someone we look up to. Like on Instagram.
Their lives are soooooo perfect.
Look at them sip their double non fat latte in a #slay mug, brows on fleek, fluffy haired dog curled up at their designer slippers. Their smile says "my life and everything in it is so perfect!" As they sigh and fall back into an oversized duvet, fully outfitted in clothes you would kill for.

Reality check!
Miss influence was likely given that outfit for free by a brand in exchange for a post about it.
Her dog just shit all over her new white carpet.
The coffee mug is full of water because she thinks she's fat.
Her boyfriend is taking the photo that he worked on staging for 3 hours and is wondering where his balls went.
That life just isn't as perfect as it seems.
So don't fret about what miss perfect is wearing. I'm sure it's cute and totally something you would love to have in your wardrobe, but I'm sorry to tell you it won't make your life any better.
You won't feel lighter and prettier and more carefree like her life looks to you. Fulfilling that impulse to buy to fill a void in your own life will only make you feel emptier.

Marketing Tricks

There is another way marketing sucks us in and has us opening our wallets faster than you can say 'BOGO' and that is scarcity!
Have you ever opened up an email from your favorite clothing store and in big bold letters it said '50% off, today only!'
OMG, you would be insane not to take them up on this once in a lifetime offer, right? SO you fill up that cart, feel proud with your mighty discount powers and wait for your package to arrive.
But wait… 3 days later another email from the same company, with another chance of a lifetime offer plops in your inbox. And then a week later, almost as if by magic, another.
You just got punked by scarcity.

Or here is another one I love. I stumble across the latest pair of nude Steve Madden pumps in size 9 on their website. Hmm… what to do?? What!? There is a little red box claiming only 2 pairs left! I MUST have these before they disappear off the face of the earth forever! *Adds to cart with the speed of light.*

Here is a secret: there are not 2 pairs left. There are thousands. Big fashion brands make millions of items so they can sell more. They just learned that creating the illusion that they are almost sold out forever makes us throw money at them without asking questions.

So what does one do?
Own only 7 black t shirts and never shop again?
Well that would do it!
Obviously that is a joke (but how great is your black t-shirt collection). I LOVE fashion. I will still buy on trend pieces and treat myself to a little 'spree' here and there. The difference is I am not buying based on comparison, impulse, low self-worth, or to try and be someone else.
I buy clothing that I will use, appreciate, actually WEAR (wow what a concept!) fits my body and suits my life.
I still drool over sexy shoes, flowy dresses and rose gold accessories, I'm human after all. I'm just not giving into every temptation to spend money I don't have in order to own things I'm not even certain that I needed in the first place.

Have you ever gotten wildly possessed at the mall and when you come to, you're stuffing 20 shopping bags into the trunk of your car?
It happens to the best of us.
My secret weapon against shopping blackout is this:

Pro Tip: If you are in a store and you find something you L-O-V-EEEEEEEE, put it down and go do ONE lap around the mall or the parking lot, or whatever! Ride the escalator, stuff your face with chocolate samples in the hallway, just spend 10 minutes moving your body away from the shop.
When the time is up, if you still NEED that thing you just walked away from, you will have the gusto to march your butt all the way back to the counter and buy it.
But 9 times out of 10, you're just going to pass.
TRY IT, it's the weirdest phenomenon!

You can do it online too! If you found something you deem as a 'must have', X the browser window, closing it completely. Get up. Go do something else for 10 minutes. Vacuum, shower, walk the dog, whatever.
Then if you have enough desperation to dig through your history folder to find the link to that thing you want, buy it. But like I mentioned before, you probably won't.

In the spur of the moment we tend to think things are a great idea that are not. Like taking that 5th shot of cheap Tequila. It was literally DA BEST idea at the time and the next morning you wanted to punch your former self in the mouth.

Physical Stress

On the subject of painful Tequila hangovers, there is a correlation between how having too much stuff has a physical impact on the body. Even if you don't THINK you have a lot of crap, subconsciously it being there is causing you a world of pain.
Headaches, fatigue, high blood pressure, and more. Lack of sleep or excessive worry about clutter (or the debt you have because of it) can lower your immune system making you more prone to colds, cause chronic pain flare ups, and even give you an upset stomach or gastrointestinal symptoms, such as diarrhea. Lovely.

Buying more than is needed, being under the weight of debt, or constantly comparing ourselves to others leads to our bodies pumping out Cortisol like no tomorrow.
Have you heard about Cortisol before? It's been in the news a lot lately because of its connection with weight gain, particularly in the lower belly, but it comes with a lot of other unwanted gifts.

Psychology today describes it best:
The stress hormone, cortisol, is public health enemy number one. Scientists have known for years that elevated cortisol levels interfere with learning and memory, lower immune function and bone density, increase weight gain, blood pressure, cholesterol, heart disease...

The list goes on and on. Chronic stress and elevated cortisol levels also increase risk for depression, mental illness, and lower life expectancy. This week, two separate studies were published in Science linking elevated cortisol levels as a potential trigger for mental illness and decreased resilience.
Wonderful. Public enemy #1, eh?

healthline.com mentions a few ways to beat Cortisol naturally. Some tips are: Be Your Best Self, Learn To Relax, Have Fun, Maintain Healthy Relationships, Stop Stressful Thinking.
While those tips are all fine and dandy, I don't know many in debt, overworked, under pressure, cluttered, taking up a second job just to pay the interest, kind of people out there who can simply apply them. They are just too overwhelmed!
Kicking cortisol's butt needs to happen before hand, at the source, by not putting these unnecessary strains on ourselves.

Waste

Consumerism has reached an all-time high, with life spans of the crap we buy being at an all-time low. I swear every time I give in and buy a $15 t-shirt, the threads unravel the second time I wear it and into the trash it goes!
Have you ever noticed how much of your stuff breaks within the first year of ownership? I'm finding myself saying cliché things like "I wish it was like the olden days when things were higher quality and made to last!" However, that cliché is true. Back in the day things WERE made to last you longer than 3 months, only that's not good business for big companies. Products are purposely made to fail, yet we line up to buy them anyway. When it does fail, instead of repairing it, we chuck it into the bin and head back over to the same company to buy a new one. What a convenient little trick on their part.
But what about the waste that has been created from this awful cycle? Who pays the price for that?
We all do.

We have demanded upon society that the goods we buy be more affordable, but we are not realizing where that cost must be made up.

So we buy and buy and buy and waste and waste and waste. Our landfills bulge as do our credit card bills.

We are at a global tipping point for how much waste we're creating and it's putting tremendous pressure on our planet. The problem with this is the average consumer doesn't have to deal (yet) with the repercussions this is having on our environment. They're happier than a clam with their newly acquired discount crap and value scoring a deal more than the health of the eco-system.

This is a cycle that does not have a happy ending.

I have a confession to make. *It's a really dirty one.*

On not one, not even two, but on THREE occasions I have thrown out a perfectly good printer because the cost for ink was more than a brand new printer (with ink). I hang my head in shame….

A scanner, photocopier, fax *(what's that!)* and full colour printer, in complete working condition, just tossed.

60 years ago the average household owning an advanced piece of technology like that would be like us owning a teleportation device (this would certainly take care of those pesky airplanes).

I didn't get that at the time. All I saw was $50 in my bank account, the ink being $60 and a new printer being on sale for $30.

I did something awful in order to put a bandage on my real problem, which was not valuing our planet and my shallow need for an item I shouldn't have been buying if I was that strapped for cash.

I wonder how many other people have done that exact same dirty deed. How many abandoned printers, cheated by the very manufacturers that made them, discarded by their careless owners, find their final resting place in garbage piles (reminds me of the movie Wall-E, there's a message in there about consumerism I think).

I could point out that in the 1950's children might have had one doll, perhaps even one ball and still had joyous, boisterous childhoods. Compared to today's kids that have a literal meltdown when they are denied the $103,840^{th}$ new must have toy.

But it's not 1950 and we have built this world of technology and innovation with no turning back.

We must learn to find that balance between lack and excess, in today's world.

3 - The Template of Life

Someone (and I still can't pinpoint who!) gave me a template on how I should live my life.
The template outlined things like going to college, being a home owner, getting a great job with a pension, and retiring in my 60's.
Sounds easy enough, right? Not too many steps, seems achievable.

Now I see that template was more like a brochure. Kind of like the ones for a 3 star resort featuring the heated pool, dinner buffet, and newly renovated rooms. It all looks wonderful, until you get there. You show up with a smile, bathing suit on, freshly applied sunscreen, all to realize you have been duped. The pool is heated with nothing more than the urine of swim up bar patrons too lazy to leave the water. The dinner buffet leaves you praying to the Montezuma porcelain gods all night. The newly renovated rooms might actually be newly renovated if the year was 1965 and cockroaches were an acceptable bunk mate.
Shit!
So you complain to the front desk, make a scene, and hopefully get your money back.

But the brochure of life doesn't offer any money back guarantees.

No one told you that:

- College might leave you with $85k in student loan debt and no job
- That starter home you bought for $390k might actually have you paying close to $1 Million dollars for it with interest and costs by the time you are mortgage free and a whole lot older.
- Your great job has morphed into more of a prison cell, keeping you trapped at it so you can afford to make the minimum payments on your credit card

- The company you just gave 40 years of your life to went belly up and your pension got wiped out along with it *(hello Sears)*
- Oh, and that now you can't retire until your 80's, unless you want to start eating cat food out of a tin

The world has gone through tremendous changes since this 'white picket fence' dream was first developed. The template of life needs an update.

HOUSING

Buying a home is something many people work really hard to accomplish! It's been imprinted on us from a young age that owning our own home means we have a place in this world. It's 'ours'. Our own piece of this Earth that we can raise a family in, cozy, free from the hectic outside world.

Get out of renting. Invest your money. Prices always go up, *right?*

Wrong.
Calculating things like cost of living, inflation, etc. your home increasing $50k in value in 5 years might not even have you breaking even.
How much did you spend on mortgage insurance, closing costs, repairs, property taxes, and interest over those 5 years? Perhaps it might be more like $70k, making your net investment in the red for $20k.

Until you own the home with no mortgage, technically, the bank owns your home. I have heard so many people say "But I OWN it" and I'm sorry to tell them 'YOU DON'T'. If you default on those payments, your nice lending company will swoop in and swiftly repossess 'your' home back.

Don't think you are the kind of person that would default on their loan? Over 1 Million people in the USA alone default on their mortgage every single year.

Also in the US, 78% of full-time workers said they live paycheck to paycheck, with 71% of all workers claiming to be in debt. Defaulting on a mortgage or feeling completely consumed by debt has become shockingly common.

Even in my home country of Canada, household debt has reached record highs. Last year, Statistics Canada released data showing that the average household had nearly $1.64 in debt for every dollar of disposable income. That makes it almost impossible to save up a nest egg or make a dent on their debt.

So is Real Estate a bad investment?

No. I think it can be a great investment, *when done properly*.

For people who have the money, know how to score a great deal, have job security and savings, great timing in the market, and especially those who intend to rent and leverage real estate as investment properties, YES. It's a good investment.

If I personally had 5 rental properties that were in a positive cash flow position, that's a hell of a good income stream. Unfortunately, only a very small fraction of the population will ever own profitable rental properties. Rental markets can swing quickly back and forth between a renters vs owners market, and suddenly those 5 properties can feel like a weight pulling you under.

Listen, I'm just personally against buying a house if I have to use debt to do it! 100%. Coming from an ex-Realtor, those are some naughty words *(I think it's against the code but who cares)!*

I literally used to pimp out overpriced real estate by the old 'greatest investment you'll ever make' line. No wonder I quit! I couldn't even believe my own bull!

We were told to buy a house young, stop wasting our money on rent, and set ourselves up for retirement! You have probably heard this from your grandparents or parents a million times over. For them, it made total sense! For a $28k starter home, I would be hard pressed not to buy into that philosophy as well. Sign me up!

But now, even taking into account inflation and current wages, starter homes are not even close to that level of affordability.

Banks spreading the message that home ownership is the only way to go is very similar to every other advertising message we are bombarded with on the daily. Don't forget, their main objective is profit, not to make your dreams come true.

Think about it like this: There is a beer commercial on TV. A guy is having a backyard summer BBQ and all his friends are there. His buddies are lining up giving him high fives as they watch girls in bikinis splash in the pool, quenching their thirst with a cold one. Suns out, grill is fired up, everyone is laughing and smiling and having a ball. Looks REALLY fun, right? What guy wouldn't want his weekend to look like that?

The beer company who made that commercial knows the mind of the average guy, so they craft targeted advertisements to entice him to buy. They do that so they can make a profit and grow a successful business. Do you think they care if he throws his own backyard BBQ shindig? They don't. As a company, they are first concerned with their profit margins and sales projections. They just want him to keep buying their product.

It would be naive to think banks are any different than this.

The 'American Dream' Example:

It's 1960. Jill and Bob are 25, in love, and they buy a home for $28k. Jill and Bob spend the next 15 years paying off the mortgage and own the home free and clear by age 40.

Bob has been lucky to work at the same paper mill since he was 15, so he has had a steady income with great benefits.

When they retire at age 60, they decide to sell the house. It's now worth $200k!

WOW! *What an investment!* What a story!

Have you ever been told a story like that? Where someone made a 600% profit on their home, never got laid off, got full pensions and benefits and lived happily ever after?

Yeah, me too, ***it's total bullshit.***

I mean, it wasn't bullshit for Jill and Bob. That was their true story! But what is bullshit is that we are expected to believe we can all have that exact fairy tale story, when it's likely only a very small percentage of us ever will.

This is what a more modern day story looks like:

It's 2017. Alison and Ben are 25 (and are also in love) and they borrow some money from mom and dad to buy a home for $385k.
Alison has an arts degree and $35k in student debt. Ben has his MBA with $90k of student debt. Mom and dad start asking for the down payment money back, because their pension went down the drain and they need the cash to retire. Alison loves the escape shopping gives her from the real world, takes full advantage of her credit cards, racking those suckers up to $40k.
They both love to entertain and this starter home is just 'Sooooooo dated', so they upgrade to a nicer place for $550k.
Ben loses his job. *Don't look away, this actually happens.*
Unable to keep up with the debt and mortgage payments, they are luckily able to sell the house for $600k, but the profits are eaten up with closing costs. They buy another house for $400k that is much smaller, but wish they had just stayed in their original home and argue about it all the time. Their debt keeps growing by the day.

OMG only 5 years have gone by in their lives y'all!
I can't even finish the story… it's too messy and ugly and you don't want to know the ending!

The modern day 'Ben and Alison' don't keep the same house for 45 years. They move. They upgrade and downgrade. In fact, they waste THOUSANDS of dollars in closing costs, lawyer fees and interest rate penalties to do this.

They won't own a house free and clear at 40, 50 or even 60, because they keep wanting a new one or borrowing against the current house to make it seem new. They will be interviewing for a job at McDonalds while celebrating their 68th birthday, when they should be on a cruise without a care in the world.
(And they were LUCKY they didn't lose their home to foreclosure or bankruptcy).

Real estate prices are not the only thing that separate these 2 couples. Spending habits and the desire to always 'buy new' makes a huge impact as well.
Jill and Bob from 1960 probably owned one kettle to boil water with for their coffee.
Alison and Ben grabbed a Kerig on Amazon, but then wanted to try a French press, and then totally splurged on that $5k built in Italian espresso machine, and then said 'screw it' and bought a cheapo plastic one from China. And still treat themselves with a Starbies here and there!
The way we compulsively spend money has a massive impact on what kind of a house we can afford.

Home ownership is NOT the best idea for everyone.

This facade that owning a home will allow us to 'make the greatest investment of our lives' is a bit of a tall tale. It comes with massive fees and costs that many people won't realize until they are completely over their heads.
They see the total cost of the house and the monthly payments, but don't take into account everything else that's hiding just beneath the surface. There are costs like repairs, taxes, insurance and bills that when all added up together, can make or break a family.
Let's say you bought a $261,000 house in Houston, Texas
I obtained some quotes and researched some public city records (just another Saturday afternoon, right?) to get a few figures to see what the first year of owning this home might cost, WITHOUT the down payment or even the mortgage payment itself!

Closing Costs: $3,700
Property Tax: $3,146 a year
Home Insurance: $1,400 a year
Private Mortgage Insurance: $2,160 a year
Utilities: $2,900 a year
Repairs: $2,500 a year

First year = **$15,806** *in extra (and usually unaccounted for costs)*

Going north of the longest, unguarded (unless that southern wall works so well they try a northern wall too) border in the world to Canada where comparable real estate is more expensive, *here is an example for a $510,000 home in Calgary, Alberta* (which also happens to be the cost of an average single family home, ouch!)

Closing Costs: $4,900
Property Tax: $4,559 a year
Home Insurance: $912 a year
CMHC Mortgage Insurance: $1,200 a year
Utilities: $2,893 a year
Repairs/Maintenance: $4,500 a year

First year = **$18,964 *in extra costs***

Hella fees, right!?
That's not even including where the heck the massive down payment is going to come from!
Or the monthly mortgage and interest payments!
"But I'm super financially savvy, I know the market, I have a great job and I can score a sweet interest rate"….. said the wall street dude in 2006 only to claim bankruptcy in 2009.

We have been sold this brightly packaged, stars in our eyes, dream of owning a home.
Have you ever fantasized that your life would be better once you had your house all perfectly set up? I did. That's why I built such a huge home, throwing myself entirely into every detail. I figured once I had the perfect living room, with all the perfect furniture, I would just wake up with purpose and excitement each day, almost as if the house would give me a new lease on life.
I was chasing that FEELING I knew I would have inside my dream home, yet it never showed up.
Is it the home itself, wood, plaster and all, that gives us happy memories with family? Or is it the people who surround us and cherishing the moments spent that really matter? I believe the same sense of belonging and achievement can happen without physically buying and owning a house.

What if owning a home is still an important dream of yours?

Look, if your dream is to own a home, ***DO IT!***
You might dream about picking out the perfect house with your family, or building a wonderful design from the ground up. Maybe it's a passion of yours to decorate and design the interior. Or you might love the thought of having a sense of stability. All of those things create wonderful feelings and memories and should never be discounted by anyone.
You have to run your own life according to your own goals, wishes and dreams.

Tips for buying a home:

- ✓ Wait until you have at least 20% of the full purchase price before buying. If you only put 5%-19% of the purchase price as a down payment, you will likely be forced to take out private mortgage insurance. It can add tens of thousands back on to the purchase price of the house, cost you more monthly and will have you paying even MORE interest to the bank.
- ✓ Buy within your means. Just because a bank says you qualify for a mortgage amount of $350,000, doesn't mean you should look in that price range. Things happen in life! Jobs are lost, family gets sick, economies can nose dive. You want to make sure you'd be able to keep making the payments if life took an unexpected turn.
- ✓ Could you go tiny? Before purchasing a house (and of course depending on your personality and preferences) you may want to consider a tiny home. Tiny Living did a study showing 89% of people living in tiny homes have less credit card debt than their traditional home neighbours, with 65% of tiny home dwellers having NO credit card debt at all! Costs for a tiny home can be as much as 90% less than the average purchase price of a 'normal' house making them super attractive.
- ✓ Don't buy for the sole reason of not wanting to 'waste' money on rent. I DON'T think anyone should only buy a house because they believe all this 'renting is throwing your money away' racket. If I could dig up the first human being to ever give that line, I am sure he worked at a bank in the housing loans department.

Why renting is my jam:

I love renting. I think renting is something people should do a little longer before diving into home ownership and massive mortgage loans. Many stories have been published in newspapers like the Financial Post and The Globe and Mail that talk about the financial benefits of renting vs buying, but the math really paints the picture.

If I took out a mortgage of **$500,000** and it took me the full term of the mortgage (30 years) to pay it off, I would have paid approx **$800,000 in payments for that home.**
That means I just gift wrapped $300,000 of my hard earned dollars and gave it to the bank in the form of interest.
If we add in things like property taxes, mortgage insurance, and repairs over the 30 years as well, **the total amount paid into the home is over $1.2 Million dollars!**
Of course renting has it's own share of costs and losses, but the point I am trying to drive home here is that a first time home buyer might not ever consider the TRUE cost of buying that house.
He was likely never told that with interest, insurance and taxes he will pay over $1 million bucks for this $500k house, and these are things that he should know.

Let's say I don't buy the $500,000 house, but I calculate what I would have spent on ONLY the interest payments to the bank and I invest that money instead.
I can turn $900/m (which is the average amount of monthly interest over 30 years that would have been going to the bank) into $750,000 cash savings at 5% interest over those same 30 years.
Yes, the amount I would have spent per month on rent would be a 'loss', but it's good to understand both sides of the equation.

Personally, I put a higher value on travel then I do on housing. I would rather spend my income on experiences instead of spending my income on the comforts and familiarity of a house.
Will I ever buy a house again? Totally. I still daydream about my 'forever' home; I'm just not even considering it until I can plop down the full amount with cash.

I don't want to give hundreds of thousands of dollars away to the bank, I selfishly (ha, imagine that, putting myself before the bank!) want to spend it on my own life experiences instead. Until the day comes when I have enough to buy a house with cash, I am going to rent. I will keep investing the money I would have spent on interest to the bank and sample different types of housing ALL over the world until I find what I like best. I don't know where I want to live because I haven't lived everywhere yet ;)

I'm practically obsessed with housing and architecture. I have bought and sold half a dozen homes in my life. One of the major draws for me to become a Realtor was the perk that I got to explore inside hundreds of other people's houses! I love looking at the floor plans, unique decor, tree lined streets. In fact, I would (and still do) find myself imagining what it would be like to LIVE in that house.

And now I get to!

I get to pick and choose different homes to live in all over the world, without the repair and maintenance bills.

Have you ever wanted a weeping willow tree in your backyard? Yeah, me too! So I will surely find a place in the Southern USA with a flowing tree in the yard to call home for a little while. What about a view of the ocean? YES! We rented an ocean front villa in Ecuador and got to leave before the salty ocean mist rusted everything beyond repair.

For me, renting is like a delicious wine tasting. I get to smell, taste and reflect on wonderfully different experiences, that I would have missed out on had I only committed to one. I have noticed myself eventually taking things for granted if exposed to them over and over again. It's like when you visit someone who lives in the mountains and you gasp "WOW what a view" from their bay window and they reply "oh, yeah... I guess I just got used to it." What a shame. You wonder how the heck anyone could ever get used to such a breathtaking sight, but it happens to all of us.

I like being able to commit to my husband, my work, my family, but I don't feel like committing to one home, especially if I am on the hook for hundreds of thousands of dollars with it! A six figure debt can really take the fun out of a situation.

"Okay Kashlee, so what are you going to do about retirement?"

Retire!

Like I mentioned above, buying a house and paying hundreds of thousands of dollars of interest is not the only way to plan for retirement. There are multiple ways to skin that proverbial cat (please don't skin a cat guys!).
Instead of forking out another $50k for a down payment, I can put that money in a low risk investment that will yield an at par or better rate than a mortgage. Instead of spending income on property tax, repairs, updating, and the immense amount of crap people fill their homes with, I can invest that as well. And who doesn't like a low risk investment?
If we do the math, I will have the same amount (if not more) at retirement than the average homeowner. And nothing is tied up in real-estate, relying on a buyer to come along and offer the right price.

I would have also had the flexibility to move to different cities, neighbourhoods, and even types of dwellings because I wasn't tied down. I can rent a more luxe place if I am having a good year and I can hunker down in a small apartment if I am having a bad year. I can roll with the ebb and flow of life and adjust to live within my means at the drop of a hat.
Some people would hate that level of uncertainty, but I call it by another name, *freedom*.

Somewhere along the lines renting got stuck with a negative stigma. It is looked down upon, usually by people who 'own' homes, which might be a distraction from their own financial problems. It's not uncommon for someone to name call and belittle others based on their own insecurities, the same way someone might call another 'fugly' because they haven't discovered their own self worth.

One way isn't better than the other, they are different. Renting, renting then owning, owning, owning then renting; they are all up to the individual and both systems rely on each other. Someone has to actually own the homes that I rent and I am overjoyed that they have the passion and desire to do so. It gives me beautiful options of places to stay all over the world that I otherwise wouldn't be able to experience. I'm just glad I don't own them.

Very similar to a grocery store! It's a great thing someone owns the grocery stores I shop in, but that doesn't mean I'm going to go out and buy one too just because I use it all the time.

So which is best for you, dear reader; home ownership or renting?

That is only a call you can make, but I hope I have debunked some of the myths and propaganda around ownership to give you a clearer idea. When I look around I see people being bullied into home ownership the same way kids are bullied into sneaking their first cigarette. Decide what is best for you. Until the day comes when the opinions of your friends pay your bills, it's only your call to make.

4 - Is Minimalism the Answer?

When I first heard about minimalism, I was immediately turned off. I imagined someone who lived in a sterile white room, with a single tiny mid-century modern orange chair, who owned exactly 2 pairs of pants, 1 notepad to scribble deep prose in and zero friends. He lived in an oversized tin can in the woods, had the very definition of a hipster beard and ate positive affirmations for breakfast.

Yeah, it wasn't for me.
I was much happier buying things I liked, going on shopping sprees, adding yet another pair of shoes to my walk in closet, picking up extra shifts to try and make an embarrassing low dent in my debt....*oh f*ck*... no I wasn't! Thankfully, I didn't have to grow a hipster beard in order to start embracing minimalism. There are no rules. I'd look pretty hot with a beard though.

According to 'The Minimalists', two dudes from the US who really have this nailed down, Minimalism is:
"a tool that can assist you in finding freedom. Freedom from fear. Freedom from worry. Freedom from overwhelm. Freedom from guilt. Freedom from depression. Freedom from the trappings of the consumer culture we've built our lives around. Real freedom."

People (including myself) have used some form of Minimalism to:

- Learn how to create instead of consume
- Relieve the pressure of debt
- Reclaim time with friends and family
- Focus on true passions
- Let go of junk and excess
- Decrease feelings of hopelessness
- Experience lasting happiness and fulfillment
- Break out of compulsive spending
- Discover more of the world

Minimalism is another way of life. It's not 'one size fits all' and it can be customized for your own personal goals.

Personally, here are the reasons I wanted to learn to embrace minimalism:

To feel lighter. I started experiencing this immediately! It's like a new corner of my mind opened up to allow more creative and positive thoughts as more and more physical junk cleared out. Items were weighing me down mentally and emotionally.

To clear off debt. I am not ashamed to admit that I spent a lot of money over the last couple years and racked up some good ol' consumer debt! But it just SAT there collecting interest, while the things I bought SAT there collecting dust… so something didn't add up.

To be more location independent. Nothing says 'stay home and go nowhere' quite like a huge mortgage payment. I feel strangely at home in hotels. I love living out of a suitcase and have no qualms about long flights to exotic locations. I always say the same thing when any vacation or adventure is coming to an end, which is: "I don't want to go home!"….so why do we then? I guess the answer is most of us have a mortgage, bills, a mile long 'to-do' list, and things that need our attention, so we must return (or so I thought). For my lifestyle, I found the removal of a permanent home and all the bills that came with it, allowed Trevor and I to travel a lot more without worry, pressure and stress. Because we are the types of people who don't need the security of one 'forever' dwelling, we found it was shackling us to a particular location more than we would have liked. Now with the removal of a mortgage, the interest on that mortgage, property taxes, energy bills, gas bills, water bills, condo fees, cable bill, internet bill, repair bills, upgrade costs and all the other delights that come with home ownership, we can travel more and not feel guilty about it!

To take back control. Being bombarded with advertisements and feeling pressured and compelled to take action on them is a shell of an existence. I don't want to be that zombie consumer, drooling all over myself, on the hunt for discount brains. I used to be addicted to that dopamine RUSH of purchasing and unboxing something new. So crisp and clean. Sigh, it felt like true happiness. That was until the chemical romance subsided 10 minutes later and the only way to get it back was to buy something else. Talk about a loss of control!

To live life on my terms. It's my life. I want to make the most of it. I don't want to limit my abilities to see and experience the world because of one too many shopping sprees. If I had known that a storage unit filled with forgotten items was costing me the equivalent of a Mediterranean Cruise each year, I would have emptied that thing out sooner! When I am an old geezer on my death bed, I won't be thinking about that Pottery Barn coffee table I went into overdraft for, I'll be mentally flipping through my scrap book of memories, picturing the wonderful adventures I had with people I love.

High Maintenance Minimalism

Learning to embrace elements of Minimalism has allowed me to do things I never thought possible, in a rather shallow way as well. Trevor calls me 'The High Maintenance Minimalist' and it's so true! *This girl likes the finer things in life!*
I will never be a backpacker in khakis checking into some eco-hut with no running water or electricity. Ever! If you want me to be really honest, it's hard enough getting me into anything less than a 3-star hotel. But just because I might be a little high maintenance, doesn't mean I can't apply elements of minimalism to my life.

I have a deep love for cool experiences, like snuggling up in a lay flat first class seat on a long flight, that I would never be able to afford had it not been for minimizing my life in others ways.

Some people think it's absolutely ludicrous to spend thousands on an airplane ticket or a private guided tour of a city and that's just peachy with me. I happen to feel the same about surrounding myself with pointless garbage.

Minimalism has given me the hall pass to spend my hard earned money on crazy life events.

It also showed me that I don't have to OWN everything I might find incredible.

If I want to take a ride in a sweet speed boat, we can rent one instead of borrowing insane amounts of money to 'own' one, just to get sick of it in a few years.

If I want to experience what it's like to wake up in an ocean front villa, we can stay at one for a month without having to mortgage myself to the eyeballs to buy one. I don't feel compelled to 'own' everything I find cool or interesting.

I'm not sure where being a minimalist became associated with being 'plain'. There is nothing plain about me, even if I do own around 5% of what I used to.

I asked advice from some savvy girl bosses about which cover photo I should use for this book. After explaining what the book was about and showing them some potentials, many of them said the pictures were too glam and didn't represent minimalism.

For a second I thought I would have to re-shoot my photos, but then I remembered something. The photos were a day to day representation of me. They were clothing I wore on a regular basis, the same makeup and hair style I wear several times a week, and quite literally my average style. I am a minimalist and this is what I look like, so to hell with reshooting anything, I didn't come this far to be put back into a mould. In their defense, they likely have a definition of what a minimalist looks like through the limited exposure about it that's been put out into the world. Someone very plain, basic, simple.

I like to think of myself as a new breed of minimalist, different from my granola predecessors. You might say I'm a bit 'naughtier' than their saintly ways.

I still consume, but I consume much less. I still waste, but I waste much less.

I have style and flair and that is okay. I choose a silk top instead of a hemp flannel shirt and there is nothing wrong with that. I've managed to eradicate debt, give up 95% of my stuff, be completely location independent and learn to live with less, so I'm not going to get hung up on what minimalists look like in the dictionary. I am that girl who might live out of two suitcases, but you can bet they are packed with selective high quality things and getting loaded on a plane to an exotic destination.

I'm still going to buy anti-aging face creams, go for overpriced massages, and upgrade my train tickets. I don't need to choose between being an in debt shopaholic or living in a treehouse with dreadlocks. Nobody does.

I've found the balance between these two lifestyles and it's allowing me to be who I really am, and that's the High Maintenance Minimalist.

The Benefits of Letting GO

Who doesn't dream of selling everything, not owing a cent to anyone and just traveling the world?? Packing your suitcase, grabbing your passport and just heading out into the horizon.

I couldn't even count how many times that wanderlust fantasy has gone through my mind, usually while stuck at work. Somewhere deep inside of me I knew that living a life of freedom was possible, even for the average Joe, and if I wanted it badly enough, it would come to pass. I made vision boards, watched 'The Secret', read 'The 4 Hour Work Week', and did everything else I could to manifest the type of life I was destined for.

To be where I am now, traveling full time with my incredible husband, being debt free and living every day with more purpose.... It just brings tears to my eyes.

Without getting to woo-woo on you, it's hard to put into words how much better I feel without so much STUFF weighing me down. It's been incredibly life changing. The kind of life changing that makes me want to sit in a circle in the park, holding hands with strangers and sing songs about it. (Only I sing like a dying cat, so I guess this book will have to do).

I used to feel like I was in a prison cell that was only 4 feet tall, making me crouch all day long, with weighted shackles pulling at my ankles and wrists. Now it feels more like my cell doors have been opened, all the guards have disappeared, and I am free to leave and explore the world as I see fit. There is a curiosity that wasn't there before; an influx of creative energy and mental stability. Even physically, I FEEL more capable and powerful in day to day life. I'm more alive, more alert, more focused. I get more done with the hours of my day then I used to in months. It's truly sensational.

*I'm not f*cking with you.*

If you would have told me in the middle of my materialism high that I would feel better without all that stuff in my life I would have told you off.
I would have chalked it down as your weakness, convincing myself you were only jealous of all the cool stuff I had and just wanted me to give it all up.
You would have been dismissed by me as a hippy quack.
Mea Culpa

I'm happy to have lived on both ends of the spectrum so I can truly appreciate the freedom of living with less. It gives me a higher level gratitude for the hard work and sacrifice in order to get to this point.

Like myself, Trevor was a HUGE doubter of a minimalistic lifestyle. He saw nomadism as being wishy-washy and found pride in accumulating stuff.
A few months before we met he was finally at the top of his mountain. He had worked for over a decade to beat a life threatening alcohol addiction, had been battling his way through an anxiety disorder and had worked his way up to a 6 figure career.
He liked having money and showing it off, buying things he never thought possible, dropping massive amounts on expensive dinners and even wearing clothing that could prove his status.

In retrospect, he saw this was his way of overcompensating for his past.

About 8 years before we met, Trevor was a homeless alcoholic, begging for change and sleeping on the streets. When his dangerous addiction almost took his life and left him hospitalized, he made the choice to get sober for good. Now that he had overcome the less than 2% chance he would succeed in sobriety, he wanted to make up for lost time. Money was his new addiction, and just like it did to me, was starting to poison his mind.

When I met Trevor I had been on my humbling journey for about a year and I could see my former self in the way we would talk about the future. "More, bigger, better…" When I first started to talk to him about traveling more, spending less money on things, he sort of looked at me like I had two heads.

Then we took a trip together. 2 glorious months in Mexico (which was like pulling teeth to get him to agree to by the way!) After that, he was hooked! It was like someone had uploaded "The 4 Hour Work Week" into his brain while he slept. He immediately started brainstorming ways we could take more adventures, rent out our condo to afford longer trips, even get off the grid a little bit.
We got engaged and then spent 6 months in Ecuador, which was another major turning point for his mindset. He began to question society, the loss of control he felt, and the boxes he had been stuffed into his entire life. Life in Ecuador was so much simpler and made him see the false prophets he'd been worshiping back home.

When we got back to Canada, Trevor wanted to start a journey into us living a more peaceful, meaningful life. We found out about a piece of land right on Lake Okanagan that had become available and we knew it was meant for us.
After one year of sacrifice and the most inventive savings plan I have ever seen, we owned the land free and clear.

Now here is the part where he could have said "Let's build a great big house where we can live forever in peace" but for our plan, that would have been two steps back. We briefly looked at house plans and prices and just felt that same pressured feeling. So we did the opposite.

January 2017, while poolside in Mexico, I said something to Trevor that I'm sure ALL couples who are on vacation say "Why do we have to go home?"
Duhh… we have a mortgage..
"Well, why do we even have a mortgage?"

DING DING DING!
In popped the realization that we truly didn't need a home or a mortgage. We just had one because it felt like the normal thing to do.

We had our home listed and sold it that week. *Scary shit right?*
And when we sold our place, we sold everything else with it. I mean EVERYTHING.
We sold house plants, picture frames, kitchen appliances, vases, rugs, art, books and furniture.
Anything that couldn't be sold was donated, discarded or recycled.

We left that condo with 2 boxes and 2 suitcases each.
The 2 boxes contained some photo albums, tax papers, and small family heirlooms. Our 2 suitcases contained all the clothes, shoes and personal items we were keeping.
All of them.
If it didn't fit in 2 suitcases, it couldn't come. (Trevor's idea)

Fast forward to today. I am writing this from inside the 1960's retro cabin that is (miraculously) still standing on our lake lot (flood of the century, blah blah blah). Trevor is working on a project inside the camper we pulled into the yard. We have zero debt. We don't have a 'home', this land is among mountains, therefore only seasonal with no winter access.
We finally succeeded in taking the plunge into freedom at a level neither of us could have fathomed.

I wanted to get another perspective on what it feels like to have gone through the same journey, so I asked my husband to summarize what he likes about his new way of life. Considering he was the world's biggest DOUBTER just a few years ago, I really loved hearing what he had to say.

Trevor: "I love the freedom to get up and go when I want. To not have to ask permission for time off, or be worried that I won't be able to make the mortgage payment if I want to go on a trip.
Having more control over my life is a major plus. I don't have to feel like a slave to banks.
I've learned that as life passes by day to day, I am always growing and changing myself. Not being weighed down by things allows me the freedom and space to roll with the punches.
I have no urge to buy things anymore. In fact, Kashlee has to stop me from getting rid of ALL my stuff. I just need a few different outfits, my passport, my laptop and my wife and I'm good to go.
Finding out more about myself in recovery from alcoholism, I've learned a lot of my urge to drink came from overwhelming anxiety. I felt stressed in social situations, hopeless about the future, and pressured by society, so I drank to numb the pain. After 8 years of being sober, I still feel anxiety, but I am finally free enough to face it and learn to deal with it. Living a life of minimalism already takes half the anxiety away and leaves my mind fresh to conquer the other half.
Even a few years ago I used to think I had to make a crazy amount of money to live a good life. That was probably because I was spending a crazy amount of money. Living with less has given me way more disposable income and has cut our cost of living way down!"

When I compare the Trevor I met a few years ago, to the Trevor I know now, it's like looking at two different people!
Seeing him be more positive, less reliant on 'things', more confident, and finally taking control over his anxiety is such a blessing.

Happiness and a positive attitude are both habits, but when we tidy up our mental and physical world, they sure are easier to practice! Letting go, clearing out, starting from scratch, getting a fresh slate… all of those things have a major benefit to our wellbeing.

A professional much smarter than I, Dr. Issac Eliaz put it best "On a physical level, strong organization means better blood flow, as well as less inflammation, hyper viscosity, and oxidative stress," he says. "This allows for the right nutrients to get to the right places, providing better antioxidant protection, which helps beat back chronic conditions from cancer and diabetes to cardiovascular disease and depression."

Hollaaa! Layman translation: Learn to live with less and you'll be a lean, mean, high functioning machine.

Waste not want not

The old adage we've all heard throughout our lives, especially from our grandmothers.
I never really understood its true meaning until this last year, likely because I didn't consider the junk and debt in my life to be 'waste'.
I thought having lots of cool clothes and drawers full of expensive makeup was the opposite of waste. More of a collection of stuff I loved, that I could pick and choose from as I pleased, that made my life better. *It was all an illusion.*
The more clothing I had, the more frustrated "I have NOTHING to wear" melt down episodes took place. The more makeup I had, for some reason, made me feel I needed even more, like somehow I was missing even better products.
The MORE I had of anything, turned into me just wanting even MORE of it. Not the opposite!

Going through my closet and being honest with myself about what I needed, gave me more clarity on what to wear. Minimizing my makeup collection streamlined my getting ready routine. I suddenly stopped wanting to shop. Sales didn't phase me. My desire for new or better things left me like a vanishing ghost.

When I stopped wasting, I stopped wanting.

Of course it started to have a major benefit on my bank account. When my thirst for spending suddenly ran dry, I noticed a major positive cash flow phenomenon. Was some good Samaritan making anonymous deposits into my account?
No, I just wasn't hypnotically buying everything in sight.
Having more money in my checking account and less charges on my credit card, made me feel even better! Once I started getting into the 'feel good' cycle instead of the 'life sucks' cycle, there was no turning back. #addicted

Which cycle do you want to be stuck in?

Have you ever asked yourself if YOUR actions are causing you joy or suffering?
Will you give up the waste so you can have joy?

Big questions right? But I really think you should read them again and try to answer them. Maybe just answer them in your head, in the notes section of your phone, or in your journal, but start that conversation with yourself.

5 - The Turning Point

I can rant and rave all day about the issues with our society, our missteps and even ways to correct it, but unless I make the decision to do something about it, nothing changes.

The same goes for you.

You might have been interested to read this book because you have debilitating amounts of debt, spend money like a trust fund kid, could star in the next episode of hoarders, or just feel unfulfilled by life in general. Absorbing these chapters one by one is a great start on the road to freedom, but it won't take you the full way there.

Decide

It's time to make a decision.
Are you going to keep ignoring the way you feel and continue down the same self destructive path? Or are you going to take action on the things that inspire you to be a better version of yourself?

The red pill or the blue pill.

I've been in the exact same spot you are in right now. I desperately wanted to feel better, happier, lighter and have a life worth living. I wanted to stop the financial rope around my neck from tightening and get some relief. I wanted to cut off the excruciating pressure to perform in a job that was sucking the life out of me. Oh yeah, and I just wanted to have some bloody fun! Book a plane ticket to a faraway land, slurp some gelato while watching the sunset and just experience something that didn't remind me of monotony.

I knew I was unhappy and I wanted to feel better, but I just didn't know HOW or where to start. Turns out that just making the decision to change and promising myself that I would take action was the first step.
So I looked fear in the eye and slammed back that red pill.

All divine intervention needs US to take the first step. Commit. Take Action.

This is your Morpheus moment, so what are you going to do??

Part TWO

Mindset

6 - Know Your WHY

Before we get into the nitty gritty of budgeting, paying off debt, saving, and eventually living a more vibrant life full of experiences, we have to take a step back into our own minds.

Learning to live with less all starts in the space between our two ears. Inside our own mind we have the power to talk ourselves into (or OUT of) any new course of action. If we can't quite see the bigger picture, it's easier to make decisions based on instant gratification that are only hurting us in the end. Kind of like my sister getting a perm for her yearbook photo, she didn't see that one coming!

You don't need to know beforehand exactly how to 'unf*ck' yourself; **you just need to know WHY you want to get unstuck.**

WHY do you want a different way of life? WHY do you want to be debt free? WHY do you want to travel the world? WHY do you want to be less dependent on material things?

Asking yourself these questions is a great way to start, as is finding out the core things in life that make you happy. I find most people want to change their way of life because they are stuck in a routine that makes them completely unhappy. Somehow the mundane parts of life seem to loop around on repeat and they're stuck doing stressful tasks instead of the things that make them happy.

We all want to FEEL better, right? But what does 'better' look like to our own individual mind?

What Makes You Happy?

A fun experiment that has always helped me when I need clarity on what it is I truly want from life is making a list of things that make me happy. The things that make me SMILE ear to ear when I think of them. The things that make my blood flow, heart beat faster and give me that tummy tickle of excitement.
Some of the things make no sense in terms of creating a better life when I write them down, but that is okay! They don't need to make any sense at all; it's just about getting them out of my head and onto paper.

Here is an example of my most recent *(and very random)* **list:**

- My husband Trevor
- My family and dear friends
- Moderate to luxury travel
- Abundance and wealth
- Success
- Teaching on my own terms
- Influence
- Learning and listening to languages
- Hotels
- First class flights
- Culture
- Inspiring others
- Being surrounded by happy and interesting people
- Giving gifts or treating others
- Finding sweet deals on travel or experiences
- Planning new adventures
- Feeling pretty and confident
- Experiences
- Being debt free

Making a 'happiness' list leaves clues. You can tell a lot about a person's priorities and personality from looking at what they write down.

Even if this list belonged to a stranger, I would have clues on what type of a person she is. She sounds like a driven entrepreneur who has a close knit circle of friends and family. She puts a very high value and importance on travel, experiences and exploration. She has a desire to share knowledge and teach others. And she sounds like she has a bit of a high maintenance side and appreciation for luxury, while still being humble and mindful of finances. If I didn't know her AT ALL, I would guess she was self-employed, and an avid traveler.

What clues do you leave in your own list?

For example, you might be working in retail now, but your list says things like, sketching designs and creating art, then you're likely in the wrong field of work! Same goes for if your list has clues like "Freedom" ,"Adventure" and "Travel", but you realize you haven't been on vacation for 6 years.

Your soul is telling you to do something about it.

WORKBOOK 1

Take a moment right now and make your happiness list. Just write down whatever comes to mind and gives you that 'at peace' feeling. No matter how abstract or abnormal it might be, just jot it down.

Study your list for a few minutes. Now write a summary of who this 'happy' person sounds like to you, pretending you just stumbled upon a strangers list. What field of work are they in? What kinds of hobbies do they have? What do their relationships look like? What does an average day look like in their world?

Does the life you are living now completely resemble the summary you made about the 'happy stranger?' What is different?

Know Your Goals & Make a Plan

It's been said that a goal without a plan is just a dream, and that saying happens to resonate deeply in my soul. There have been many moments in my life where I have known pursuing a specific dream would have made me happy, but I had no goal and no plan, so it just stayed as a day dream and nothing more.

One example is playing the piano. I have always dreamt about being able to sit down at a piano, touch my fingers to the keys, and have a gorgeous melody fill the room. Every time I see a piano in a restaurant or someone's home, I imagine myself being able to play that exact one with confidence and passion. Instead I play an amateur version of chopsticks.
So what has stopped me from being able to play?
Myself. Not making a goal and a plan on how to get from point A to point B.

It may seem like such a small dream in life, but I know this to be true: "How I do something, is how I do anything." Meaning, if I can let something as small as playing the piano pass me by, what bigger things in my life am I also sabotaging?
Without making a goal (destination) and a plan (the map to that destination) I will only ever daydream about it and wake up one morning, 95 years old, and it might be too late. *Here's hoping to wake up at 95!*

My Goal: To be able to play Debaussy's Clair De Lune for Trevor on our 2nd wedding anniversary.

I made the goal very specific. It wasn't just 'play the piano', I opted for a certain song that has meaning to me. Leaving it up to chance might have me playing 'chopsticks' instead of a great classic. I also gave the goal a deadline. We were married July 2nd, so that gives me an end date to plan my strategy within.

The Plan:

- Research piano teachers in the UK, Vietnam, Malta, Italy, Canada, and anywhere else we will be living for the next 2 years.
- Consult with them to find out approximately how many hours of practice I would need in order to play a song of that skill level.
- Take the total number of hours estimated and divide it by how many weeks are left until my goal date of July 2nd.
- Let's say that equals 1 hour a day, 3 times a week. Now I know I should be budgeting and planning out my work schedule to allow for 3 hours per week of piano lessons.
- I can go ahead and book those teachers!

An easy to follow plan meant keeping the end goal in mind and reverse engineering the tasks that would get me there.

Making a clear goal and a fully thought out plan, I have now made a dream of 'being able to play the piano', into an action based system that will have me sitting down on my anniversary and playing a beautiful song for my husband. I know all the steps that will get me there, the costs, the time involved and I can see the end goal in my mind so vividly.

This exact same formula can be applied to ANY dream, no matter the size or complexity. Your dream might be to quit your office job and work from home, homeschool the kids in a foreign country, lose 50 pounds, learn a new language, build your own website… it's completely up to what makes you happy.

WORKBOOK 2

Make a goal and plan for 3-5 of your dreams that mean the most to you. (Hint, if you look over your happiness list again, it may give you some inspiration).
Then on the 'Goal' line, make a specific and clear goal for that dream. Bonus points for an end date.
On the 'Plan' line, write down the specific tasks that will need to be completed to get you from where you are now, to your end goal.

(Example)
Dream: "I want to keep my job, but be able to do it from home"
Goal: Convince my boss they should allow me to work fully from home, starting 'goal date'.
Plan:

- Research other companies that allow remote working in my field
- Do 'x' and 'x' projects from home in my spare time to show them I am productive outside the office
- Create a pitch business plan in powerpoint showing the benefits
- Draft up an agreement that will protect both parties
- Schedule a meeting with them Dec 15th at 4:00pm to formally pitch the idea.

7 - Take Action

Talk it Out

Plans get REAL when you talk to someone about them. There is something about releasing words into the physical world and having someone else hear them that makes it all more likely to happen. Talk to your spouse, your bestie, your dog or your imaginary friend about your goals, plans, and what you are going to do about it first! Journaling is a great way to talk to yourself, but try and get some actual conversations going with the people in your life.

Having your spouse on board is a major plus, but don't get down in the dumps if they want nothing to do with this new way of life you have been raving about. Many people need to come to terms on their own time and face their demons when they are good and ready. If you find your spouse being particularly unsupportive, just keep doing what you're doing and know eventually they will come around.

Decide on one or two core people in your life that you will start to share your new ideas with and see if they want to make some positive changes with you.

ACTION

Nothing happens without action.
You might as well light this book on fire right now unless you intend to take any action towards the life you want to live.

Ghandi said: *"The future depends on what you do today"*
He didn't say your future will depend on what you think about potentially doing one day. He said **TODAY**. *Are you going to ignore Ghandi!?*

No one in history has ever been truly 'ready' to do anything. But many great people just took action anyway and learned as they went.
Without inspired action, we would have nothing.
Nothing ever would have been invented, created, written, composed, built or erected. The only difference between notable people who have created wondrous things and the average Joe is ACTION. The average Joe has just as many dreams, thoughts, ideas and inventions' sitting deep down inside of him, but his inability to take action is what keeps him average. Sorry Joe!

How to take action:
Step One: Just. Do. It.

There is no 'how to' guide on taking action because that in itself would be some form of action. You just have to do it and not psyche yourself out before you even get started.

Look, taking action (especially in to new and unchartered waters) is super scary and I get that, but what scares me more is NOT ever taking action and living a life full of regret.

Once you do start to take action towards your goals, you will notice something amazing happening. It's one of the best feelings in the entire world: making progress.

When you start to get back data on your results, even the tiniest bits of progress, you will feel like a million bucks. The chemical reactions that happen in the brain from making positive progress are stronger than any 'instant gratification' highs we could ever get. Progress gives us a sense of accomplishment, achievement, confidence, and high self-esteem that we can't get from anywhere else.

Whether you start to take action on your deepest dreams, or simply take action on your junk piles at home, you will be propelled forward with an insane amount of energy and momentum when you start making progress.

WORKBOOK 3

What are some things you have been procrastinating and avoiding taking action on?

Write them down along with ONE action item that you will put into play in the next 30 days.

Listening to Others

You want to take back control of your life, finances and goals, but there is still something that's been rattling around in your head. *"What will people say??"*
It's a completely legitimate fear to wonder what your peers might say or think when you are all of a sudden pinching pennies and selling your stuff online. After all, most of us make the mistake of letting the opinions of others dictate our self-worth.

My thoughts on this are:
Until the opinions of others pay my bills, or put millions of dollars into my savings account, I can't let them dictate my life.

Misery loves company. Any person that makes a smart ass remark about your goals or plans is completely envious and likely battling with their own low self- image. They are jealous and the last thing a jealous person wants to see is a peer succeed while they stand still. You cannot be responsible for their small way of thinking, nor can you try and change their opinion. I'll bet you $100 that they are in debt themselves and are pissed you have decided to take action instead of them.
Just keep doing you and greatness will follow. All you can hope for is that your actions might inspire them to make a change in their own life as well.

Change is hard and requires sacrifice, and there are times that sacrifice might come in the form of who you socialize with.
It's been said countless times that we are the sum of the 5 people we spend the most time with, and I couldn't agree more.
If I am always hanging around with people who are broke, unhappy, always complaining and blaming everyone for their problems, I'm likely going to act like a fool as well.
On the other hand, if I am surrounded by driven, accomplished, positive people who support the people around them, I'm going to be a much happier and successful person.
When I was in Real Estate, I hung around with a lot of people who started drinking at 10am, talked badly about their spouses and hated going home.
Guess what happened?

I found myself pouring that martini a little too early, taking my partner for granted, followed by one too many late nights. It was the first time in my life I started to understand how much my social circles were impacting my life.

After that little 'quarter life crisis' I made a point to surround myself with top shelf people as often as I could. I don't necessarily mean only uber successful Fortune 500 CEO's, I am talking equally about people with good character as well.

Looking around at the people in my life over the last 5 years, these words come to mind: driven, compassionate, loyal, creative, thoughtful, courageous, dynamic, abundant, adventuresome and consistent. I can see some of the characteristics I admire in my close friends and family, rubbing off on my own personality.

Ask Yourself: Who are the 5 people I spend the most time with? Do they have qualities and values I admire? Or are their priorities very different from my own?

Fear & Excuses

These two words: 'One Day', have the power to steal your entire life from you. **Deep right?**

But unfortunately it's true.

At some point 'one day' will turn into never, and it was only fear and uncertainly that caused that to happen.

I beg of you, do not let that be your unhappy ending.

Have any of these thoughts run through your head before?

"I don't think I could"
"What will my family think"
"I don't know where to start"
"But I have kids"
"I'm not like you"
"It's not a good time right now"
"Maybe next year"

I've had more than my fair share of these tricky little excuses contaminate my brain before. They are made by FEAR in order to hold us back from our true potential. Fear will make us second guess ourselves any chance it gets. Fear implants thoughts of guilt, shame, comparison, low self-worth, and even anxiety about what other people think of us. Fear needs you to keep believing its lies for it to exist, so it's quite invested in making sure you are buying all its bullshit. It's the master of manipulation, tangling you in a web of false truths.
Fear will take your whole life from you, if you let it.

At some point in my life, the pain of staying the same became greater than the fear of change, and that is when some amazing things started happening!

Recognizing our fears has a much better impact on overcoming them than just trying to ignore them. We fear something because we are uncertain of the impact it might have on us, like failure, for example. But failure doesn't really exist. Each time I have ever 'failed' in my life, it was actually a crucial lesson that I needed to learn in order to grow. It actually added wisdom and value to my life.

Identify what you are afraid of, what's holding you back, and then tell it to BEAT IT!

I have a friend who is extraordinarily talented, I mean she has a natural ability that she was born with, but always let's fear get the best of her. It's been a lifelong dream of hers to start her own business that will allow her the freedom to also travel a lot, since the two are actually closely intertwined. Year after year, she never takes the next step. Sure, she writes things down, makes goals and business plans, even buys domain names, but never pulls the trigger.
I recently asked her what has been holding her back this whole time, and she simply responded "I'm terrified I won't do well at it". Appreciating her honesty and vulnerability in telling me that, I still had to respond with "Right now, you're not doing well with it.
At all.
In fact, you are basically living out your fear every single day.

If your deepest fear is that you won't do well with it, guess what babe, you are doing crap with it now and you're still alive. For five years you have held back due to fear and that's caused this business to never 'do well'. So in knowing you have already experienced your worst fear, the biz being a flop, can you get over the fear and actually try?"

She looked at me like I just opened an alternative dimension right before her eyes. *She was completely stunned.*

After about 5 minutes of navigating her way through this new perspective, she said back to me "I almost told you off, but you are completely right! I live every day like this business already HAS failed and I feel the pain of the failure even though it's never actually happened."

That pain is what kept her from launching her business, because she figured if it hurt that much before even trying, she would be in for a world of pain later on. Only, she never considered what making even 1% progress would feel like, which would feel immensely better than the pain she was feeling.

I'm happy to say that I've seen her take more action on her business idea in the last few weeks than I have ever seen her take in the last few years. Once she realized she was actually living a daily repeat of her own worst fear, she had little trouble pushing it to the side and getting shit done!

WORKBOOK 4

Take a moment to think of some fears and excuses you've been held back by lately. *Write them down.* Look deeper into why you are holding onto all the pain associated with those fears and excuses. *Jot those down as well.*
Is it worth carrying them around? Or is it time to let go?

8 - Need vs Want

Need vs Want is a subject that has its own chapter because it's the biggest lesson to learn for a more balanced life.

Thinking you need something when you don't is what causes your credit card to balloon. It's also caused you heartache and regret when you thought you NEEDED that abusive partner in your life.
Not being able to tell 'need' and 'want' apart has essentially caused 80% of all the problems in your life. The bad relationships, the collection agency calls, not being able to find your keys amongst the mess, the procrastination, the horrid outfit choices and even much of the overwhelm you feel day to day.
We all have needs and they must be met to ensure our survival. Maslow figured this out a long time ago. We need a roof over our head, food in our bellies, clothes on our bodies, but that doesn't mean the house should be a mansion, the food caviar and the clothes Givenchy.

The very definition of the word **NEED** is: a requirement, necessary duty, or obligation.
A lack of something deemed necessary.

Now let's look at the definition for **WANT**: to feel a need or a desire for; wish for.
to crave, demand, or desire. to be without or be deficient in.
to fall short by.

Ew! To 'fall short by'… that is not the kind of feeling I want driving my shopping habits. *It sounds, well, kind of pathetic!*
I think it's still important to have desires, goals and wishes in life, just not under the illusion that it's deemed a 'need'.

Repeat after me: **I will identify the difference between what I NEED and what I WANT.**

Trust me, I know how much a 'WANT' can feel like a 'NEED'! I have had many moments in my life where I NEEDED those shoes, that car, those blender attachments and that crop top with the tags still on it from 5 years ago.

75% of the crap you spend your money on, you do not need. Not even close. And as much as you think you 'like' it, you won't miss it after you stop buying it all the time.

Like daily coffee runs, magazines, cable TV, eating out all the dang time, random home decor you're certain will make your life better, that 7th bronzer you now own, the list goes on and on and on.

It all adds up to DEBT. Or at least money that could have been spent on memories, experiences, and seeing the world.

Look, I get it. I go weak in the knees for a good Sephora binge, but let's put things into perspective here.

Confusing need vs want sucks the money out of your account and the life out of your soul. *(What a drama queen)*

I'm not saying we should all become hermits, never going out, cut off our social life, and just stop buying everything completely. I am saying that from personal experience I know cut backs can be made and actually IMPROVE your day to day life.

Let's say I was buying 2 bottles of wine a week, sit down dining once for lunch and once for dinner per week, grabbing the occasional drive thru once a week, spending about $90 a month at Sephora and on other health/beauty things, buying around $200/m worth of clothes, shoes, and any trendy things I want, and let's say another $100/m on random shit like throw pillows, or books, or workout gear, or whatever!!!

Did you know that equals $10,152 a YEAR y'all!

And let's add Cable TV onto that *(+$840/year)*
Or what about Starbucks 4 times a week *(+$680/year)*
Fake nails once a month *(+$720/year)*

Eye opening, right!?

All I can say about this is STOP the madness! Just stop getting your coffee out and make it at home. Stop drinking 2 bottles of wine a week and just have a glass or two on Friday's (your waistline will thank you too). Stop buying clothes and makeup that sit around and collect dust. Do your own nails. It's honestly like an addiction and once the haze of insanity lifts you will thank me!

How to cut down habitual spending:

Take yourself off ALL those daily or weekly emails that want you to shop. Out of sight, out of mind. You are not going to miss out on anything. If and when you actually NEED something from one of those stores, you can go to their website and see what the deals are. Every company has some sort of deal going on at all times. Pro tip: If you install the chrome extension 'Honey' to your browser, it will automatically find coupon codes for ANY shopping site worldwide and apply them for you, making sure you score the best deal. HOWEVER, don't have it running full time on your computer or you will feel the urge to shop when your brain gets high from the coupon code Kool-Aid. Just turn it on when you actually need to buy something (example: You need a new bra. That is a need. Might as well get a killer deal on it)

Make stuff at home. Coffee at home (and you don't need a Nespresso machine to do this). You'll get even higher points for making ground coffee the good old fashioned way compared to the single serve capsules. Coffee pods cost between $0.49 to $0.89 a cup, but choosing ground will cost around $0.23 a cup, saving you an average of $400 a year.
Have friends bring over food for potlucks instead of dining out all the time. You can hear each other talk, be more present, and won't want to die after getting another $120 dinner bill.

Make a hard RULE to not buy ANYTHING until yours is 90% gone. I used to see someone on Instagram raving about a mascara and then next thing I know my bathroom drawer was full of seven different mascaras.
WTF? Mascara is mascara.

I just need ONE tube. One, not seven. So now I do this thing where I actually just use the dang mascara I bought and I wait like a rebel until I notice it starts to get a little dry. Then I go to this thing called a store (or Amazon) and I buy its (one) replacement. Genius! Who knew we lived in a world where we could easily and quickly restock on everyday items! Here I was stocking up on mascara like it was the makeup apocalypse. RIP to all the stuff I bought too many of and ended up throwing away.

If you have something like it already, you don't need another one. If you have a blender you don't need another blender. If you have a pair of black leggings you don't need another pair of black leggings. If you have 5 pink bags, you don't need another pink (or any colour for that matter) bag. Chances are you are not being photographed daily by the paparazzi that are going to write about your wardrobe repeats, so no need for endless variety. When we went to sell everything in our house to become fully nomadic I was slapped in the face with how many 'doubles' I had.

Here are some of these things I found:

- I had 2 nutra bullets and one Ninja blender. Have I ever found the need to blend 3 different things at the exact same time? No. (Cocktail party anyone?)
- 4 of the exact same sized cooking pots (out of 10 pots total). Considering I don't really cook, WHY!
- 3 copies of the film Twilight. Two of them were on DVD and 1 was on Blueray. I should also mention I own it on iTunes, which kind of makes four copies. That totals over $100 spent on a movie I can watch for free on Netflix. Also, don't question my taste in movies.
- 6 pairs of black heels. I know, I used to be a former shoe fetish person and to many of us 6 pairs of a black heel sounds reasonable, but it's not. They were all the same: closed toe, matte, identical heel height.
- 4 leather jackets, 3 empty hard drives, 2 old cellphones and a partridge in a pear tree.

F*ck cable. Seriously. Get your news online, watch sports with friends, binge on the cheaper option Netflix and save yourself a ton of cash. Cable sucks anyway. It's full of loud commercials, shows you don't even like but get sucked into and have you seen the package prices recently? If you want sports, some Nat Geo, a few movie channels, you are likely in the $150-$200/month realm. Or to put it another way: You could actually buy killer seats AT the sports game instead of a year of cable.

Stop drinking so much and save yourself the hangover and the money. I love wine a lot. My husband is sober so if I am going to drink it at home, it's usually going to be alone. That just doesn't have the same 'pour me another glass' ring to it, does it? I actually love the fact that I spend a lot of my time around someone who doesn't need to drink to have fun. It's taught me how to abstain and still have a great time AND save money. I still drink when I want to, usually more with friends, but the point is I don't make it such a centre of my life anymore. It has given me more money for other things and not constantly nursing a wine migraine makes me a heck of a lot more productive. *It can't hurt my waistline either.*

Just think before you buy "would I rather go to Italy, or buy this instead?" When I got in the habit of comparing the REAL cost of an item, it helped me decide if I truly wanted to buy it or not. I'm sure we ALL want a brand new outfit, or Botox in our foreheads, but if it comes at the cost of missing out on a lasting life experience, no thanks.

WORKBOOK 5

1- Look at your last 90 days of bank statements. Make a list of all the things you would honestly deem a 'WANT' and *add them up.*
How much did you spend on things you didn't need in the last 90 days?

2- Next, beside each 'want' you spent money on, **write down a free/cheap alternative.** It could be as simple as 'refrain' or you could get creative *(ex- instead of buying that book, getting it at the library for free)*

What if you had a 'check-stop' to make sure the purchase you were about to make was a good idea. A necessity check list if you will. Each time you feel compelled to buy something, I double dog dare you to put it through this filter:

1. This purchase fills a need in my life

2. This item will be purchased with money I already HAVE and not money I need to borrow

3. In one year, this item will still matter to me

4. This item has more value to me right now than saving the money would instead.

MIC DROP!

When I started applying this filter to my own life, I immediately stopped making a ton of impulse purchases because it really put into perspective what I NEEDED vs what I wanted in that moment.

Try it yourself.
Better yet, store it as a note in your phone, and consult it before you make a purchase.

WORKBOOK 6

Get out your last 30 days of credit card bills and bank statements. *(Or you can do 90 to get a bigger picture)*
Write down the purchase under PASS or FAIL after you take it through the 'check-stop' filter test on the previous page.

PASS:

FAIL:

It's good to learn what makes something a 'need' and a 'want' long before we are actually standing in line at the cash register.

I'm not smart enough to make one of those snazzy flow charts you can visually follow, but these are the same tips I would have put on there:

How you know you NEED it:

- ✓ It nourishes your body
- ✓ It's part of your daily hygiene
- ✓ You wear it on a regular basis
- ✓ It's part of your job
- ✓ It's part of your vital studies or personal growth
- ✓ It keeps you warm or cold
- ✓ It has a purpose, utility or value in your daily life
- ✓ Your Grandma would have one

How you know you WANT it, but don't actually NEED it:

- You think it will make your life better
- You don't want to miss out on not getting it
- You already have something similar to it
- You are feeling sad and it looks happy
- You are compelled to buy it after seeing an ad for it once
- You're comparing yourself to others
- The urge to buy is coming from a place of lack
- Your grandma definitely doesn't have one

You can see the difference as clear as day in the two lists. The 'NEED' list comes from a place of necessity, growth, health and usefulness. The 'WANT' list comes from a place of lack, low self-esteem, sadness, and self-medicating.

The occasional treat

What about the occasional treat, you know, because 'you deserve it'. Does that mean you can throw all this Need vs Want advice in the bin?

Yes, when it's actually occasional.

When I first started watching my weight, taking my health into consideration and learning about healthy eating, I also learned about the CHEAT MEAL!

This glorious meal of the week where I could smash my face with any delectable dish I saw fit. Apple pie with pecan ice cream, deep dish pizza, nachos with extra cheese; every week a new indulgence! A few months went by and I realized that I wasn't gaining any weight from my weekly cheat meal, I was still advancing with my fitness goals, and everything looked dandy. A hangry little voice inside my head seductively whispered: *"go ahead Kashlee, have TWO cheat meals this week, you deserve it."*

Somehow I managed to further negotiate with myself that four cheat meals a week would still be a good idea.

What happened next? The top button of my jeans wouldn't do up, so I had to fold the waistband down and wear extra-long shirts for a while. I felt lazy and tired and my skin broke out in sugar acne. I was lethargic and self-conscious.

But whyyyyyy, I thought I deserved it!

That is the problem with self-policing. We are masters at pushing the limits and giving into our desires.

So yes, you can still just buy things once in a while just because you WANT them, but perhaps you should establish how often 'once in a while' is, and a budget to match.

Some examples:
- Maybe every time you hit a milestone in your business (like every 100 new clients), you treat yourself to a $100 item.
- Or if you were able to save an extra $200 that month, you can frivolously spend $50 as you see fit.
- One of my favourites is: If I can sell some of my unused items, 50% of that money can go to buying something I want. It's great because it might make me get rid of 5 dresses in total and I get to buy 1 dress without dipping into my savings at all.

WORKBOOK 7

Set up some reward systems for yourself.

(Example)
"I can spend 'x' however I want with zero guilt when I accomplish 'x'

It's not about perfection

I still find myself getting caught up in a whirl of emotions and buying things I don't need. What has changed is how frequently that happens. A few years ago I would estimate I gave into temptation and spent money on something I shouldn't have **at least** a couple of times a week. Add that up over a year and it might equal 100-200 transactions that I had buyer's remorse from. *(Or worse, thousands over a lifetime)* Being nomadic definitely helps this cause, but I'm not totally immune! I would say maybe a few times a month I cave, but I sincerely believe it's a healthy way to balance out life.

I'm not perfect and I will never be, because perfection doesn't really exist.

I will be the first to admit that I will absolutely buy another pair of uncomfortable, super trendy shoes that don't even fit me right, just because they caught my eye in some shop's window. I know I will fill up my Amazon shopping cart and wonder **"WTF am I going to do with a Star Wars Tupperware set?"** (The answer is 'be the coolest girl in the universe, that's who'.)

Need Vs Want isn't about seeing who can live with less, or who can be the perfect minimalist. It's about learning to control desires and not let insecurities make our financial decisions.

80/20 rule.

Pareto's principal essentially tells us that 80% of the time, we are only using 20% of our belongings. And it's SO TRUE. *Pareto really knew his shit.*

Take a quick mental inventory of what you use on most days. Think about what you eat, the clothes you actually wear, the items you use. I bet you use the same things, about 20% of everything you own, over and over. You likely wear 20% of your own closet or use 20% of your makeup 80% of the time. 20% of your friends are the ones you talk to 80% of the time. Even 80% of the meals you cook probably use 20% of all the ingredients you have in your cupboards.

I always see proof of this principal when I do laundry. I find I am always washing the SAME sweatshirts, the same panties, and the same workout clothes over and over each week. If I added up every item of clothing I owned and divided it by what was always in the hamper, I bet you it would work out to 20%.

That 20% of stuff you use 80% of the time is NEED.
The 80% of stuff you have and use 20% of the time is WANT.

Knowing that Pareto's Principal is a real thing, how much longer will you hold onto (and to continue to grow) the 80% of things you own that you don't need. It's a vitally eye opening theory to wrap your mind around. When you can actually identify the 80% of things in your life that are just sitting around, it's much easier to justify letting them go.

Trevor and I went ahead and cut out that 80%.
We went through all these same exercises and identified the 20% of things we used all the time. This made cutting out the 80% a considerably easy task.
Surprisingly, nothing is actually missed. Most of it we weren't even using at all!

Security Blankets

Many people hold onto their excessive amounts of 'things' because it makes them feel better. They associate control, power, variety, and worst of all safety, to having lots and lots of stuff.
There is nothing 'safe' about not being able to pay your bills and having your home repossessed.
Social security blankets are also at play here. Trying to keep up appearances, impress others, boost self-confidence, self-worth, or status. Again, it's a war that's impossible to win. Someone will always have more and the root of the problem has been covered up with shiny new toys.

When purchases wrap you up in comfort, just like a security blanket, it can easily blind the difference between want and need.

I know I used shopping and brand names as security blankets in the past. I always wanted to have the latest and greatest or something shiny that would impress, just so nobody would notice how poorly I thought of myself.

It's like when a magician diverts your attention elsewhere so he can perform his trick in plain sight without anyone seeing. I felt that if I could hold the attention of others on the things inside my home, or the clothes on my body, that they wouldn't see my sleight of hand.

Sure, it made me feel better for a few minutes, I mean who doesn't love people complimenting and cooing over your possessions. But in the end it just left me with overwhelming credit card bills and a lot of fake ass friends who didn't truly know anything about me.

Know that you ARE enough without the brands. You are a vibrant, wonderful, powerful being that is better than the things you surround yourself with. These items don't define you, your actions do.

People will remember how you treated them over what you wore or how your decor was arranged. Work on your biggest asset - YOU - and it will be more rewarding than impressing people with stuff neither of you can afford.

Learning to let go of security blankets will take practice, time and patience. If you do have emotional attachments or insecurities about parting with things, start slowly. Once you get rid of a few unneeded items, you WILL start to feel better and it will give you the confidence to continue.

WORKBOOK 8

1. Write down the last 10 items you bought that you didn't really need.

2. Let's find out WHY. Think about why you bought it, how you were feeling, or what mindset you were in at the time for those 'want' purchases. Did you buy the item to escape, distract yourself from pain or stress, etc.

3. Take your top 2 reasons for buying items and think about how you could solve those problems at the source.

Printable & Editable Version at traveloffpath.com/workbooks

Personal Development

Personal development was a key tool in discovering my value. Come to think of it, I can't name ONE wild successful person who doesn't consistently work on their own personal growth.
Working on yourself doesn't have a set start and end date, as we are always changing and facing new obstacles that are foreign to our frame of reference. Take Tony Robbins for example. He is one of the most famous life coaches in the entire world and has already successful people pay him over $1,000,000 a year for his guidance and growth lessons. Major names like Oprah, Nelson Mandela, Leonardo DiCaprio, Bill Clinton, Princess Diana, Maria Menounos (my fav human!) and even Mother Theresa have hired Tony Robbins to help them continue to evolve throughout their lives and careers.
If someone as accomplished as Oprah benefits from personal development, I think we could all use a little too.

I've made it a habit over the last few years to include at least 15 minutes of personal development into my daily routine. That might be a few pages in a book (which I love to highlight and dog ear for easy access to good ideas later *(NOT recommended with a library book)*), listening to a podcast, hearing a TedTalk presentation, watching a video, or journaling my gratitude's.
Reading is by far my favorite way to absorb personal development, but podcasts are great when I don't have a lot of extra time that day. I can easily play and still listen to the content when I am putting on makeup, folding laundry, or even cooking a meal.

Personal development falls under the NEED category. We all need and deserve the knowledge and tools to be the best possible versions of ourselves. I have included a list of my favorite personal development books, videos and tools in the resource section located at the back of this book.

Part THREE

START

9- Let's Make A Budget

START!

Doesn't that sound so productive already!?

This chapter is all about taking action, stopping the flow of mindless spending, paying off debts and getting control back of your finances (and mind!) We are also going to trim the fat, declutter and organize your life and make a solid foundation for the future.

Basically, *we are going to kick some major ass on your bills.*

First we need to see what we're working with.

Making a budget, a true honest budget, is a great way to see what's really going on with your finances. It's hard to know where you are headed, if you don't know where you are coming from. Writing out everything you are earning and spending tells the full story in black and white. This story might be messy, depressing, and eye opening, but don't worry because you're going to make a revised one later on in this book that's going to rock your world.

It's important to write down what you are REALLY spending on things so that later on, we can actually see how much progress you have made.

Let's start with how much income you have coming in.

WORKBOOK 9

Your Income:

Salary or Pay – after tax: *(also referred to as net income)*
Monthly & Yearly
=

Spouses/Partners salary or pay – after tax:
Monthly & Yearly
=

Other income:
Monthly & Yearly
=

Total income:
Monthly & Yearly
=

30 Day Snap Shot Budget

We are just going to take your last 30 days, or an average of what you would normally spend, to get a snap shot of your payments, expenses, bills and other outgoing cash. Not all of these will be a monthly expense but man does needing new tires sneak up on a person!

The essentials (in no particular order)
Mortgage/Rent:
Property Tax:
Condo Fees:
Repairs/Maintenance :
Electricity:
Water:
Heat/AC:
Cable:
Internet:

Phone/Cell Phone:
Home/Renters Insurance:
Groceries:
Cleaning Supplies:
Child Care:
Pet Care:
Gym/Fitness:
Car Payment:
Car Insurance:
Car Maintenance/Repairs/Oil Changes/Tires :
Fuel/Gas:
Parking/Tolls:
Public Transit/Cabs:
Essential Clothing/Shoes:
Toiletries/Makeup:
Medications/Prescriptions :
Hair Cuts :
Health Insurance:
Life Insurance:
Office/School supplies:
Student Loan Payment:
All Credit Card minimum payment:
Other loan/debt re-payment:
Personal growth/education/advancement:
Charities/Tithing:
Gifts:
Investments/Retirement:
Savings:

Essentials Total =

The extras
There are always extras! I have done this whole budget thing before and I would just jot down $200 under the 'miscellaneous' category because it sounded about right. Or maybe it was because I was hoping if I said $200 it would somehow change the fact I was really wasting more like $1000 on extras each month.

I purposely did NOT put a 'fun money' or 'miscellaneous' section into the Essentials budget because I don't want you to make the same mistake I did. Instead, here is a list of alllllll the extras I could think of so that you can REALLY see what the miscellaneous number is. Again, just use your last 30 days or a general average, as some of these expenses won't be every single month, but you know best where your money is usually going.

Movie rentals/Movie theatre:
Alcohol/Wine:
Video games/Games:
Tickets/Concerts/Events:
Bars/Happy Hours:
Restaurants :
Fast Food:
Starbucks/Coffee:
Bakery/Treats:
Magazines/Books:
Subscription Boxes/Services:
Mani/Pedi:
Eyelash extensions/Waxing:
Hair Dye/Blowouts/Extensions:
Spray Tans/Tanning:
Massages/Facials:
Home Décor:
Music/Sat Radio:
Valet/Cover Charge:
Uber (when not needed):
Parking tickets/Fines/Late fees:
Apps/In-app purchases:
Online Shopping:
Meal Prep/Grocery Delivery:
Lottery Tickets/Gambling:
Jewelry/Handbags/Perfume:
Clothing/Shoes/Trends:
The dreaded going over cellphone data:
Hotels/Flights/Trips:
Bank account fees:
Boutique Classes (hot yoga, etc) :
Smoking/Vaping:
Shipping/Delivery:
Storage Unit:
Dry Cleaning:
Housekeeping:
Supplements/Vitamins:
Random ATM withdrawals:

Extra's Total =

Budget Check

1. Take the total amount of income and subtract the ***'essentials'*** total.
= $

Are you spending more than you make on the essentials?

Yes: You need to focus on downsizing, and creating a secondary stream of income.
No: Good on ya! Living within your means is a powerful thing.

2. Take the total amount of income and subtract the ***'essentials'*** total, then subtract the ***'extras'*** total.
= $

Are you spending more than you are making on the essentials and the extras together?

Yes: You need to stop the outwards flow, cancel unnecessary things, make sacrifices, sell your used stuff, etc.
No: Great. Not out of control. Is the number big enough for you to pay off any debts with, save for the future with, etc. Do you want a bigger number?

Debt Totals

Consumer debt:
Student debt:
Other debt:
Car debt:

Total Debt Owing: $

Knowing the total amount of debt you have is crucial to making a plan to pay it off. For right now, we are only going to look at your total amount of debt, because the next few sections of this book will give you tips on how to make some serious dents in it.

10 - Get out of debt

The first step in getting out of debt and making your money stretch further is to stop the FLOW of charges. When you cut off the amount of cash that is flying out of your bank account each month, you immediately feel some financial relief. It's kind of like having a small hole in an inflatable pool toy that is slowly making it deflate. Patching it up and stopping the loss of air will keep you afloat.

Let's identify where you are losing money each month, so we can stop any more money from escaping.

Fine Tooth Credit Card Comb

Just like dust bunnies under the bed, long forgotten reoccurring charges have set up shop on your credit card. I'm talking about charges you might not even know are there because you started a subscription eons ago and just haven't really noticed since.
The first step in debt freedom is to STOP these charges from happening again and tighten incoming bills.

When I did my first comb through, I was surprised at how much crap I had on there that I didn't really use, or it wasn't worth the price to me. But it was so easy to just say "oh, it's just $9/m, that is so cheap" but when you have 20 of those things billing you, WOW does it add up quickly!

I had *(in Canadian Dollars)*:
Ipsy $21/m
Fabletics $65/m
Netflix $13/m
iTunes $14/m

Naturebox $25/m
Scribed $13/m
Dropbox $15/m
iCloud $5/m
BOD $10/m
Wired Mag $40/y
Travel & Leisure Mag $40/y
FitFabFun $230/y
Amazon Prime $80/y

That works out to $2,482 a YEAR! *pardon me while I pick my jaw up off the floor*

As much as I love trying new products, Ispy and FitFabFun crap just ended up in cupboards, I wasn't using half of my music or ebook subscriptions, I had 2 'cloud' subscriptions when Amazon prime offered free photo/video/file storage, and well, $2,482 could have put me in a swanky beach hotel for a week or two.

After cleaning up my act I now only have: Netflix, Amazon Prime, iCloud (smaller), and BOD - working out to only = **$380 a year.**
(I don't miss anything I cut out. At all)

WORKBOOK 10

1-Round up your credit card, debit card and PayPal statements for the last 12 months. 12 months is KEY here because there are many charges that only happen once a year (like Costco for example) so you want to catch monthly and yearly reoccurring charges.

2-Highlight ANYTHING that is a reoccurring charge that is not a vital service (like your mortgage, car payment, electricity bill, etc). Usually its things like subscription boxes, music services, magazines, memberships, etc. After you have them all highlighted, write them down in the **first column** of this workbook. *(Just write each specific charge once, example: Netflix will just go down one time, and not 12 times if you get charged for it each month)*

3-Next, use the **second column** for how much that service costs on a monthly basis and the **third column** to tally up what it's really costing you for 1 year *(example- my iTunes music subscription sounded like a steal of a deal at $14/month, but when it works out to be $168/year, it somehow seems like less of a bargain.)*

4-Assess what the heck you are paying for. Is it worth the yearly cost? Do you use it? More importantly, does it bring VALUE to your life? In the **forth column,** put a big **'X'** beside the services you know you should/can cut out of your life. *This doesn't mean forever, but just for now.*

5-In the fifth column, add up the amount the services you can cut off cost and tally (both monthly and yearly) at the bottom. This will give you a bigger picture of just how much savings it will equate to. Make a monthly and yearly tally for everything you are cancelling THIS month. *I will be saving 'x' per month: I will be saving 'x' per year:*
(Does that number surprise you?)

6-Make a TO DO LIST. Re-write down the services you are cancelling and a deadline to have them cancelled by within the next 30 days. Keep this list somewhere you can see it, or set reminders in your phone to complete it! If it feels like a large list to complete, task yourself with cancelling one or two subscriptions a day until your deadline. Once you get the hang of it, you'll be looking for other subscriptions you can cancel because it feels so good!

Printable & Editable Version at traveloffpath.com/workbooks

Move Debt Around & Start Crushing It

If you are anything like me, my husband and I had this one credit card that we both put charges on and then kind of pretended like it didn't exist. We would throw $100 at it here and there to cover the minimum payment, but kept it out of sight and out of mind. Then one day we looked at it and said: *"Oh my how you've GROWN!"*...and at 20% interest it was costing us a ton.
Like, **around $2,000/year in just the interest alone!**

Obviously paying that bad boy off ASAP is wise, but there might be other options to help in the meantime. Some credit cards will offer you a 0% (or maybe even 0.99%) interest rate for 6-12 months if you transfer your balance over to them, instead of keeping it with the bank it's at now.

I had another card that was offering 0% interest on balances transferred over for 12 months! That meant I could tackle that massive $13,000 credit card balance with $0 in interest over 12 full months which really helped!
I saved $2,000/y by switching that credit card balance to a 0% promo, which would have just gone into the banks pockets. Or in other words, that one simple move bought a roundtrip flight and 2 week stay in Bali. That should motivate you to do the same!

You may not have another credit card that will allow you to do a balance transfer, so in that case, dial up your current card and negotiate a better rate with them. You can mention you are thinking of transferring the balance and closing the account, so if they would like to keep you as a customer, they need to offer you something worthwhile.
Even a 5% rate cut from 19% to 14% is better than nothing! If you don't get anywhere with the representative on the phone, ask to speak to a supervisor.
Trust me, they want to keep you as a customer!

WORKBOOK 11

Write down how much you currently have on your credit cards *(each one if you have multiple)*

How much interest are you paying per month on each card *(your last statement will tell you, or you can calculate it yourself using the interest rate)*

If you transferred the largest balance (or a few balances) to one card and received 0% for 12 months, how much interest would that save you over the year?

ACTION: If you have another credit card that has a zero balance, OR has a low enough balance to receive a transfer onto it, call that card company right now. Ask them if they have a 0% balance transfer available for you to use. Negotiate that promotion for 12 months, but settle at 6 months if you have to.

ALTERNATIVE ACTION: If you don't have another credit card you can transfer the balance to, you can:
(A) Apply for a new 0% interest rate credit card.
(B) Apply for a new low rate credit card.
(C) Ask your current company if they will lower your current interest rate
(D) Apply or use a personal line of credit that has a lower rate than your current credit card. Your bank would rather you stay on as their client, at a lower interest rate then have you declare bankruptcy and possibly never get their money back.

Highest Rate FIRST!

After you do any potential balance transfers and rate negotiation, it's time to make a plan of attack on the debt that is left over. The best rule of thumb for this is to pay off the debt with the highest interest amounts first, which are usually credit cards.

I have heard advice that you should pay off your smallest debts first, because it will give you a sense of satisfaction and progress, but that doesn't actually give you more money, it's just a warm and fuzzy mind game. If you are cool with pulling up your britches and not needing the extra validation, you can make a bigger impact on your debt.

Priority #1 - Bad debts, high interest

Debt that has no asset tied to it and whopping interest rates should be crushed first. They are the most risky. Credit cards, store cards, payday loans, high interest unsecured loans. Usually over 10%.

Priority #2 - Medium interest

Debt that has a moderate interest rate but also might have something to show for it. A car loan is a great example of this. Once your bad, high interest debt has been fully repaid, start attacking this debt next.

Priority #3 - 'Good' debt, lower interest rates

Good debt is kind of an oxymoron but let's go with it. This type of debt usually has an asset worth more than the balance owing. A mortgage, home equity loan, small business loan, or even student loans. Once all bad and moderate debt has been paid in full, you can focus on these debts, as they are most commonly the largest and will take time and strategy. Your mortgage isn't something you are going to be able to pay off in a year or two, but after all other debt is gone, you can certainly start doubling up on payments!

11- Let Go & Downsize

When I went over my spending habits, I realized a lot of it had to do with the space I was in. A big walk in closet just screams out "FILL ME!!!!", doesn't it? And hey, you might want to keep your walk in closet, and that's cool, but if you are broke as a joke and want to see the world….well… that's what you'd call 'priorities'!

It seems to be human nature to compulsively fill the space we inhabit, no matter how big or small. If I moved you from an 800 sq ft apartment into a 1,800 sq ft house, chances are you would grow into the bigger space and find a way to fill it up in no time.

Downsizing can be a great way to save money, lessen your responsibilities, free up time, and even make you re-evaluate the way you live day to day.
When you get yourself into a smaller space, you will find you'll also adapt to the size quite naturally.

Downsize Your Vehicle

Less than 10% of North American homes don't have a car, but that number is on the rise for the first time since the 60's. Car share apps, UBER, enhanced transit and the high cost of car ownership has a lot to do with this.
If you live in a metropolitan area, you likely have access to public transit that costs a fraction of what a car payment, insurance and gas will take from you.
At the end of the day, a car is a depreciating asset and is NOT an investment.

What if I approached you and said: "Okay, I have the perfect investment opportunity for you! It will only cost you $30,000 and there is a 100% chance you will lose money on it, most of which will happen in the first few years!" *You would tell me to get bent.*

I know that vehicles are an incredible convenience and for most families a vital part of day to day life, but this idea is worth exploring.

Could you downsize to a less expensive vehicle?
If you have a secondary vehicle, is it absolutely necessary? Did you grow up in a one vehicle household? Our parent's made it work, why can't we?
Do you need a vehicle at all?

A great way to answer these questions is to put the cost of owning the car into perspective.

- Add up your car payment, car insurance, average gas bills and repairs. (Monthly and annually.)
- Figure out how many days or how many times a day you use the car in a month.
- Now find out how much taking an uber, a car share, transit or a car pool would cost you for the frequency that you now use your current vehicle.
- What is the difference in monthly and annual costs?

For some people this number is staggering!

I asked a friend who lives in Toronto to do this experiment and see what her situation looked like. She is married, has 2 kids who are in elementary school and both her and hubby work downtown. They both have separate vehicles.
Her car payments, insurance, repairs and average gas worked out to be around $910 a month or $10,920 a year.
When she added up what taking the occasional Uber, the subway, carpooling with friends, getting a ride with hubby, etc. that cost came out at around $450 a month.
A monthly transit pass is $140 a month or $3 a ride.
A car share is $10 an hour or $79 a day.
Uber was around $20 a ride.

Even if she took an Uber daily for 50% of the month, bought an unlimited monthly transit pass and hired a car share for the entire day, twice monthly, she is saving HALF the money she's currently spending on her vehicle. That equals out to $5,000 savings a year, which could be going to debt, savings, or family vacations!

Would you sacrifice owning a car in order to save thousands in a year?

When you downsize your vehicle, or get rid of your car all together, it might mean you can instantly save money in other areas of your life, like housing. You might be paying for an expensive parking spot in your building or renting one in the city. So many people felt the need to buy a house with a single or double garage, solely because they needed it to house their vehicle. If you don't have a need for the garage any longer (or maybe such a large garage) there might be an even more substantial savings in store for you.

Downsizing Your House

Some people have a major emotional attachment to their home, and that is perfectly okay! Others find their home to be a source of stress and unwanted pressure, especially if they are living in a place bigger or more expensive than they should be.
Big homes (that are unneeded) just mean bigger payments, more money spent to fill it with furniture and decor, bigger heating, cooling and electrical bills, bigger property taxes, and more time or cost to clean.

We owned a condo but soon figured out it was a pain in our neck while we traveled and we were only home about 4 months of the year. Each month we were gone, we were 'double spending' because we still had to pay the mortgage, condo fees, property tax, bills, etc. It was costing us around $1,700/m (or $20,000 a year!) even when we were not there! **So we sold it!**

I know our example is extreme, and not everyone wants to sell their house to travel full time, but we sure did!

Now without the $20,000/year in house bills, we have extra money to travel. AND yes, we still put plenty away for retirement for all the worry-warts who ask. Remember, real estate is ONE way to prepare for retirement, but it's not the only way. It actually used to be a great way (says the former Realtor) but that has changed for the average family. More and more people are getting into mortgages way over their heads, changing houses every few years, borrowing against the equity, and so on. Owning a home with a huge mortgage still owing on it come retirement is NOT a good retirement plan.

If you don't want to sell your house and become full time nomads like us, that doesn't mean there isn't still a great opportunity for you to downsize and save big time on living expenses.

Are you currently living in a home that has unused rooms, too much extra space, or is just costing you too much monthly?

Going back to Pareto's principal (The 80/20 rule) studies show us that 80% of the time, we are only using 20% the space in our home.

A question to ask yourself is:
Do I need a home this big? Or this expensive?

Yes, I want to stay in my current home:

Look for ways to save money on bills and energy costs

Free ways:
- Take shorter showers
- Use smaller lamps and desk lighting instead of turning on all lights
- Sleep with the house a few degrees cooler in the winter and warmer in the summer
- Turn off electronics and lights when not in use
- Utilize natural sunlight instead of electric light when possible
- Only run full loads of laundry
- Air dry or line dry clothing instead of using the dryer
- Wash dishes by hand instead of the dishwasher
- Unplug the garage or basement fridge

- Keep heat registers clear and unblocked from furniture
- Set your hot water heater a little lower

Ways that cost some money, but are worth it in the long term:
- Add extra insulation to the attic
- Seal up drafty windows
- Replace old bulbs with new low energy ones
- Tune up the furnace and replace filters
- Replace worn weather stripping
- Use energy star appliances

Look for income opportunities

Even if you need all the space in your home, you might have some opportunities to make some extra cash. See if you can rent out parts of your home or yard on a month to month basis. These are all just ideas and might not be adhering to your insurance requirements or local bylaws, so do your own due diligence.

Basement Suite or Room for Rent:
Go over what the fair rental value for your suite or room is and make sure you are charging accordingly.

Unfinished Basement:
You might be able to get someone to help you finish it for a cheap price if you give them discounted or free rent in exchange for doing the labour. They get a place to stay and you add to the value of your home.

Garage or Storage:
A 6x4 storage facility can cost up to $200/m depending on the city! Consider renting a similar secure space in your garage or basement to someone for much less.

Parking:
If you have an extra parking space in your garage for a car, or even driveway space for an RV or other type of vehicle, you might be able to rent it out seasonally for someone in need!

NO, I want to sell/stop renting my current home:

Great! If you don't need all the space, that particular area, or just want something that doesn't cost as much, you can really make a difference in your budget and your life! A smaller or cheaper home will not only save you money on bills, it will also save you TIME. So much time is spent cleaning, fixing, tidying and maintaining a big home, and freeing up more time is priceless!

Get a price:

If you own your home, have a Realtor come over to give you a free analysis on the homes market value. Speaking from experience, a good Realtor should be able to establish a very close estimate on how much your house will sell for.
This might also help you discover if there is any equity in your home, which you can use for a down payment on something smaller, put into savings or investments, or clear off massive debt with.

See what else is out there:

No matter if you will be renting or buying, research what rental or purchase prices are in your goal area. If you are moving states, provinces or countries, make sure you know about differences in property taxes, condo fees, utilities, etc.
Make sure you can find a suitable place that is lower enough in price to make a big difference on your monthly and yearly expenses! Try adding up the total yearly cost on a few different options so you can see the big picture over the next 5 years or so.

For the hardcore downsizer:

There is no shame in living full time in an RV, tiny home, cabin, VW van or anything else your heart desires. Did you know that the CEO of Zappos (who is also a multi-millionaire) lives full time in his Airstream trailer? Smart guy!

I have seen more well-to-do people making the choice to live in their retrofitted vans and buses than I can count. These people aren't 'homeless' or 'transients', they are people who want to take control back over their lives and do what feels right for them.

The other day, there was a post in this all women travel group I am a part of that totally brought this point into perspective. A woman who was tired of paying $3,800/m for a San Fran apartment and feeling overwhelmed by her $120,000 in student loan debt, decided to say "F*CK IT" and live in her SUV. I should also mention this woman is a lawyer who loves her job, has a well-rounded social life, and is super fit to boot. With her SUV abode plan, she will crush her student debt and make a substantial amount of savings in just a few years. It's not her plan to live in her SUV for the rest of her life, but it's the action she is taking in order to set up her future for success.
Last time I checked the post it had around 600 comments of other women from all walks of life posting pictures of THEIR vans, cars, buses and RV's that they called home. Other comments included swapping tips, funny encounters, and lots of people asking for advice on how to also live in a car.
This is quite the movement!

People are sick and tired of being told what to do and how to live. The 'normal' way of life has been crippling people financially and finally they are taking a stand against it!
If you want to live in a bus, do it up! Also, make an Instagram so I can be inspired by you on the daily!

Like I mentioned before, when Trevor and I reside in Canada, we live in our RV. It's all we need. It's allowed us the freedom to travel like we do, and when we are home, it keeps the cost of living down even more. Is it small? Yeah, it's pretty compact, but so are all the condos under $1 Million in Vancouver, New York and San Francisco *(and our RV was a teeny tiny fraction of that cost!)* It's not 'roughing it' by any means. It has a queen sized bed with foam topper, full size closets, big shower, electric fireplace, flat screen TV, surround sound system, outdoor kitchen, work area, and a lakefront view. All the creature comforts without the mortgage.

12 -Declutter & Sell Your Old Crap

This next step can make downsizing an actual reality when you realize how much STUFF you don't need in your house/life.
For some reason this tends to be the HARDEST step for most to put into action, but it's the single most freeing and rewarding one to accomplish. If a former materialistic maniac like me can do it, so can you!
All of the following will mean diddly squat unless you just DO it.
It's so easy to say 'next week, next month, next year' and that is exactly how we wound up with piles of crap surrounding us. Just get er' done!

Now that you have cut down incoming expenses, and determined 'need vs want' it's time to clear out the old crap and make some cold hard cash doing it.

Step 1: Revisit your 'Want vs Need' workbook
The first step on your decluttering journey will be to ask yourself when faced with any object: "Do I need this?" OR better yet "Does this bring any value into my life now? Does it serve me?"
My socks where knocked RIGHT OFF when I discovered how many of my once treasured items and mistake purchases did NOT serve me or fulfill a need whatsoever. I was merely holding them 'in case'. *In case of what?* I wanted to open a professional garage sale of crap?

Step 2: Start in the drawers
Or the closets. Or under the stairs. Or anywhere that doesn't see the light of day a whole bunch. This is where the jackpots are hiding! Huge boxes full of crap that you have even designated as 'not good enough to be out in the house with the rest of the crap', labeling it as sub-par crap. 99% of what is in these dark chambers can be donated/sold/thrown away. No, I will never need that old DVD player, the 20th pair of mittens in the house or that old textbook from 20 years ago.

I went like a hurricane through our condo and our storage unit.
I found DVD players, sealed makeup, brand name clothing and shoes, handbags, a DSLR camera I didn't use, old TV's, artwork, furniture, kitchen appliances (namely that KitchenAid mixer I 'HAD' to have but never took out of the box) and countless other items.

Step 3: Make 4 piles
Take a room, or an area of the house that won't drive you bonkers to do this in (although that might light a fire under your downsizing ass) and make 4 piles. *1- Sell. 2- Donate. 3- Trash. 4- Keep.* I found these piles magically grew and shrank and items migrated between them over and over again as I tried to reason why I needed that thing I don't need. In my opinion, the piles should be as big as their order listed above. 1 should be HUGE, 2 should be pretty hefty, 3 should be decent and 4 should be microscopic.

> SELL Pile

Sell your stuff online! It's free and easy and fast!
Facebook buy/sell groups are incredible for this. There are hundreds of ravenous fiends waiting to get their next used goods fix. You literally will join a local group (for us it was Kelowna Buy/Sell) and you will list your item, the price, some photos of it, details, and pickup info. If you price the items right, they will fly off the shelves. My advice: Don't get greedy, just get it over with. They can be extremely time consuming if you are trying to always get top dollar. You can also use sites like Kijiji, Craigslist, eBay etc. Or of course, ask someone you know if they want to buy it. As you are raking in the cash and the adrenaline is pumping, it's wise to set a goal or a designation for all that money. It will keep you incentivized and focused on the task at hand. *Example: I will take my husband on a 1 week vacation to Mexico. Or- I will pay off that credit card bill of $2,000.*

> DONATE Pile

When you can, donate to people near you.
I mean locally as well as socially. It's amazing to be able to donate something to someone and see their smile, watch them use and appreciate it and know it's still a part of your community.

Example: we donated a color printer, school supplies, white boards and kitchen items to a teen studying to be a chef! It's great to watch someone grow and excel! We also made donations to charities, shelters, and local food banks.

Look up places that need donations ahead of time and keep a list of when you can make drop offs, or even better, if they do pick-ups. Get your donate pile out of the house once a week so you can keep the flow and momentum going.

> TRASH Pile

Some things are not suitable to be sold, nor donated, so the trash is the only place you can put it. Listen, if you are tempted to keep something that is so unwanted it cannot be sold or donated, you are literally holding onto garbage. There is a show for that called Hoarders…get rid of the trash before you have your own episode. Look up your local recycling regulations to see what can be recycled instead of black bagged.

> KEEP Pile

Keep going through this pile over and over again, because your first reaction to many things will be "KEEP! Duh!!!" After you have combed through your keep pile at least 10 times, all remaining items must have a home assigned to them. Find a spot for them where they can be organized and put to use in your everyday life. If you find yourself putting them back into a box under the stairs, you likely don't need to keep them after all!

Step 4: Start going through everyday items

After your work has been completed in the garage, under the stairs, in the drawers, etc; it's time to attack the things you see every day. The clothes hanging in your closet, small appliances on the counter, and the more prominent items in your home.

This one was harder to do, but I kept remembering: WANT vs NEED. I combed the closet over and over again and kept asking myself "When was the last time I wore this?" If it was over a year and it wasn't a specialty gown, it HAD to go in Piles 1, 2 or 3.

Step 5: Talk about the BIG things

Have a conversation about the house, the car(s), all the big ticket items in your life that come with matching big ticket payments. I got rid of my Mercedes that I didn't drive more than 2 times a year but was costing $900/m (ouch!). Not everyone wants to sell their house like Trevor and I, but here are some things to ponder: Do you use all the space you have? Could you sell and buy a smaller place for much less money? Do you have 2 vehicles and really only need 1? Are you making large payments on things you don't use like a snowmobile, boat, etc?

Step 6: Plan for the future

Talk about being accountable to each other for buying new things going forward. Only purchase it if it serves a purpose and adds direct value to our everyday life. Example: If my laptop is getting scratched and I want a sleeve for it that would be alright. If it's not getting scratched and I am not using it ever and I just SAW a sleeve I like because it was cute.... no, that is not alright.

So was this easy? There were some moments where I temporarily felt like I was going to have a panic attack and then it just faded away. It's not EASY, but neither is hanging on to crap for no reason while your credit cards grow and loom over your head constantly. This is much easier than the awful feeling of weight on your shoulders.

My last little tips for your downsizing journey:
- Use smaller things (forces you to give up excess!) Smaller make-up cases, smaller storage areas, smaller closets.
- Do you have a double of an item? (like 2 toasters or 2 identical Lululemon shirts?) Then one of them is 100% going in pile 1-3.
- Storage? If you have a storage locker somewhere, I challenge you to get the smallest one they offer and make it work
- If you have debt, mark at least 75% of all your 'sales' to re-paying this debt. 25% can be used for fun stuff and instant gratification thrills, but the debt needs to GO!

- Involve your spouse and do it as a team. Make it fun and keep each other accountable! Trevor pointed out SO many things I didn't need and I wasn't even aware of it.
- When you can, try and sell your items to locals. Having to ship things you sell on sites like eBay and Poshmark will take up time and money.
- When selling things online, take really clear and bright photos and make sure to be detailed in your description. It can make your items stand out against the competition.
- When people are looking for an item in a Facebook buy/sell group, they post 'ISO', which means 'In Search Of'. Let's say you have a old record player you want to sell, try searching for people who have posted that they are looking for one BEFORE you post your listing of the item. You might find a buyer this way first.

Now here is where some people say "I don't really have anything to sell!"

Yes you do.

Invite me over and I guarantee I can find hundreds if not thousands of dollars just sitting around in boxes that you didn't even remember you owned. (Omg, reality TV show idea! Producers…call me.)

Keeping things around that have no use for you are only causing you pain. They take up mental and physical space, you may have debt you could be paying off with the cash you earn from selling, or you could be doing something a lot more fun than sitting amongst your boxes of stuff.

WORKBOOK 12

What part of the house are you starting your de-clutter and sell project in?
What is your deadline to have everything in that area sorted?

- Bedroom Closets
- Front Hall Closet
- Linen Closet
- Kitchen Drawers / Cupboards
- Bathroom Drawers / Cupboards
- Under the stairs
- Basement
- Garage
- Attic
- Under the Bed
- Book / Media shelves
- Storage Unit
- Living Room
- Dining Room
- Bedrooms
- Family Room
- Other room / space

Write down a list of things you can think of off the top of your head you can sell *(and an approx. price of what you think you could get for it)*

You might start the process of selling your old stuff and get completely caught up in a whirlwind of emotions like I did.

I get it, the thought of selling your stuff can give you instant anxiety, right? That gut wrenching, nauseous kind of feeling?

It did for me too! Actually, when I first started downsizing, I kind of cheated! *(hear me out)*

I started putting things into a big storage unit instead of actually selling them. It was kind of a 'test run' to see if I would spontaneously combust or not.

Well guess what... I didn't cease to exist when my prized possessions were tucked away and the world continued turning. But in the process I was wasting $170 a month (That's $2,000 a year BRO!) on a storage unit that was acting like a halfway house for my crap.

If I could go back in time, I would have NOT added that stage into my downsizing journey, since it ended up costing me $6,000 over 3 years. (Yes, I still cry a little at all the flights I could have taken!)

However, I realize that everyone is different and we ALL have different levels of attachment to the things in our lives. That being said, here are my 4 universal tips to effectively breaking up with your stuff, sans the ice cream eating cry fest.

#1 - Is it lust, or love?

SHOES. I loved shoes. I still love shoes. At the height of my materialism madness I actually had 95 pairs of shoes. My relationship with shoes was definitely in the 'lust' category.

But what happens with all relationships built on lust? They fizzle out. So many of the pairs of heels I hoarded only gave me that 'I must have you' feeling for a few weeks and then once the rush was over, I never looked at them again. There WERE however a few pairs that I LOVED. I took them out to dinner, dates, galas, events, or for that perfect Instagram shot. About 5 pairs in total were always my reliable 'go-to's.

ADVICE: Nobody needs a late night calling, lustful relationship in their lives. Notice the things that are only giving you short term happiness and then leaving you feeling empty. Break up with them! It wasn't meant to be in the first place.

Keep your 'in it for the long haul' BFF objects.

#2 - Are you using it, or is it using you?

Imagine you had a boyfriend and he didn't have a job, never contributed to anything and just sat around the house like a bump on a log. Would you keep him around?

Probably not.

But there are things JUST like that hanging around your house, that you've actually spent MONEY on, yet they just sit there giving you nothing in return.

ADVICE: If it gives you value, is a tool in your life, gives utility to your day, or even makes you smile, KEEP IT.

If it just wants to sit around taking up space and not contributing to your life, tell it to hit the road. (Ooo, and better yet, SELL it to finally get some money back out of that freeloader!)

#3 - "But we've been through so much together"

I know right!? You spent so much time thinking about buying it, you stalked it for a while online, and you even spent WAYYY more money on it than you should have. Now it's time to reassess your relationship with it, but you are clouded by all the memories and effort you took to get it in your life.

ADVICE: Just like people put deadlines on working their issues out with each other; put a deadline on that 'Thing'.

If you don't use it in the next 6 months, it's time to say goodbye. No matter what it said to you on the receipt, it's over.

#4 - True love does exist.

Sometimes you just KNOW.

There are things out there that are irreplaceable, unique, one of a kind, and give off that kindred spirit kind of vibe.

These are the types of things you might want to keep in your life.

If you cannot buy it again, replace it, or it doesn't feel right in your soul to part with it, then don't. Things like family heirlooms, keepsakes, stuff you will pass down to new generations, or items that just make you happy or give you joy.

ADVICE: Be realistic with your feelings. If it's an item that could easily be purchased again if you desperately needed it back (like a book, movie, shirt, couch) then you don't need to stay dearly devoted to it now. But if it's something that you can't put a price on, find a way to keep it in your life and don't hide it away.

WORKBOOK 13

Your sheet to keep track of sales

As you start to list and sell your used items, you will want to keep track of things like pending sales, pick up times and amount it sold for. *(The printable and editable spreadsheet is best to use. Download it here)*

Item to be sold:

Asking price:

Pictures taken?:

Posted in:

Pending sale:

PICKUP/DELIVERY time/place/name:

SOLD and GONE (with final price):

Tally of money made:

Printable & Editable Version at traveloffpath.com/workbooks

PART FOUR

Plan and Save

13- Saving & Investing

Look at you go, you debt squashing, soon to be sipping Pina Coladas in the Bahamas, bad ass!
Now this journey is more than halfway done, it's time to shift our gaze into the glorious future.

Saving!

Whoa, whoa whoa…don't let your eyes glaze over, this is important stuff here. I promise to not put you to sleep. Read on.

I personally think its wacko to try and save while you still have debt, so this should only apply after you have taken care of that dirty business. When the bills are smaller and there are no extra payments going into interest, you start to notice money is much more attracted to you.

How much money should I be saving each month?

Experts say between 10%- 20% of your pay check should go right into savings. Excuuuuuse me! While that is great advice, CNBC reported this year that half of Americans are still living paycheck to paycheck, making this almost impossible!
Many of the tips and exercises in this book should have freed up more income for you to save, but you still might not be at the 10-20% ratio yet.
Don't give up all together. Start saving what you can, when you can and it's better than saving nothing at all.

Auto Save

When left to our own devices, we tend to spend money instead of save it. The best thing we can do is remove the temptation as early as possible and automate the savings process. Many banks have a feature that will automatically save a % of your pay. Try setting this at 5 or 10% and see how it goes! If you don't seem to notice much of a difference, raise it to 15 or 20%. This takes your savings out right on payday so you are much less likely to blow that cash.
Some employers have an option to do this as well.
If you can't manage to auto save even 5% of your pay, **can you do 1%?**

Round Up
Many bank accounts have a round up feature you can take advantage of to maximize your saving efforts. It will 'round up' your debit purchase to the nearest $1, $5 or $10 and dump it directly into your savings account. An example is if you had it set to the $10 round up and you went and bought a $6.75 lunch. The system will round the purchase up to $10 and place the extra $3.25 into savings for you. Most people won't notice such a small round up and after a while you will have a little nest egg built up from everyday purchases.

Blast from the past
If you did your homework in the last few chapters, then you would have started cutting down a ton of debt and therefore the amount you spend monthly on interest as well.
But what if you pretended you didn't?

Let's say your old credit card (that you have now transferred over to a 0% card) was costing you $215 a month in interest.
If you could survive with that amount being charged to you then, maybe you still can.
Now that the $215 isn't going to the bank in the form of interest, try putting the same amount into your savings account instead!

Same goes for anything you sold. You used all your 'I just decluttered my entire house and sold all my crap' money to pay off debt, and if you have some cash left over, stick it in the highest interest savings account you can find.

Make it a game
Everyone loves a good game! Make a cool change jar out in plain sight, a family swear jar everyone contributes to (big money in this!), a colourful thermometer chart, even an app to keep you motivated to hit milestones. We have a summer home in Canada on the lake and are lucky enough to have immediate family right next door to us. Between the 3 families and 3 properties, we find every weekend is a party. We even turned that into a savings game! Every pop can, bottle of water, beer, or wine bottle is saved up and recycled for a refund. When you have dozens of visitors every week, they sure add up! We all throw it in a big pot to save up for something amazing that will benefit us all, like a new BBQ or a holiday feast!

What am I saving for?

The future. None of us know what tomorrow is going to look like. In order to ensure we won't end up in a real pickle, we all need a safety net.
By putting away a % of your income on a regular basis you will be saving for things like: emergencies and unforeseen expenses, repairs and maintenance on your assets, healthcare or accidents, retirement, and to HAVE SOME FUN!

All this debt crushing, minimizing, downsizing and saving is a real party pooper if there isn't an element of excitement thrown in there. You need to have a 'FUN FUND'. All work and no play is not a way to exist and thrive on this planet.
A big wad of my savings ends up going towards travel (big surprise). My personal philosophy on money is: You can't take it with you.
I will never NOT live life to the fullest because mayyyyybe I should just leave it in the bank to be a 'good, safe, respectable member of society'. That's not my jam.

I am responsible, but I'm also not going to let adventure and experience pass me by!

For this reason, I have THREE savings accounts!

1. Emergency Fund *(aka 'shit happens' fund)*
2. Bucket List Account
3. Everyday Fun Account

Emergency Fund
Emergencies are called such because they are things we didn't plan, see coming, or expect to happen. Sometimes insurance will cover certain emergencies, but many of them will come out of our own pocket. Having a fund that you DO NOT TOUCH unless it's dire should be mandatory.

Some examples of things that you are saving up for: Higher than normal tax bill, important big ticket car or house repairs, ambulance bills, hospital or doctor's bills, vet bills, unforeseen dental or vision care, funeral costs, job loss or career change, replacing a lost phone or computer, lawyer retainers or legal costs, unexpected travel, identity theft, unexpected pregnancy, helping a family member in crisis, divorce, natural disaster, relocation. Side note: a sale at Sephora is not an emergency. The more crap you have and the more financial pressure you are under, the bigger this account needs to be. The experts suggest having enough money in your emergency fund to cover 3-6 months of your basic expenses (rent/mortgage, groceries, gas, etc.). If you lose your job, you'll need to cut back on entertainment and eating out until you get another paycheck coming in. Looking back at your budget from Pillar One, how much money would you need to save for a 3-6 month emergency?

Bucket List Account
My favourite savings account! I fill this sucker up and empty it out as often as I possibly can. This is where the nectar of the gods resides!

It feels SO good giving up something like a $120 mani-pedi when I know I will be $120 closer to island hopping in the Caribbean.

If you are like me, a dedicated travel savings should be implemented so you have something uplifting and rewarding to contribute to. Sacrifices always seem worth it when I get to spend that money jet-setting to a faraway land and being immersed in a new culture. I really can't think of anything better to spend my hard earned money on.

Everyday Fun Account

Life on a budget doesn't have to be so stuffy! This account is for the smaller, more frequent and everyday things you want to save money up for. They are expenses that are equally balanced between being social and being responsible.

Some examples of things you are saving for in this account are: Date nights, attending weddings, giving gifts to others, hosting a dinner party, treating an old friend to lunch, sports, social events and seminars, fundraisers, field trips, etc.

Will having 3 savings accounts cost me anything?

Check with your bank, but no, it shouldn't. All three of my accounts are free to open with no monthly charges, as well as one free monthly withdrawal. I can however 'transfer' as much money out of these accounts as I need to, as long as it's going to my checking account, or to pay the credit card I also have linked with that company. This way if I wanted to book a flight and pay for a hotel with my 'Bucket List Account Savings' I can transfer the funds I need without penalty.

INVESTMENTS

The one thing I really didn't want to get deep with this book, is investments. I am not a financial guru and 'the right way to invest' is a pretty complex and sometimes abstract thing. It differs from person to person and is heavily dictated by your tolerance to risk, preferences, budget and personal needs. One thing I can tell you with certainty, you shouldn't be thinking of investing unless you have all your debt paid off. Your debts interest payments will eat up any profit you might be making in the stock market game, and nobody needs a party pooper like that around!

Investing your money and saving for retirement is an important part of life that many don't consider until it's too late. Unless you want to be working to the ripe old age of 88, you should start your retirement plan ASAP. The sooner you start, the more money you will have come your golden years. The compound effect is a wonderful thing!

How to invest your money

Stocks - These are shares of a company you can purchase, and of course, hope they increase in value. Stocks are relatively easy to self-manage in the sense that you can set up an online trading account and buy them yourself.

Bonds - Bonds are basically this in a nut shell: you loan a company or government money they need, and they promise to pay you back. This is done with regular interest payments and then finally with the original principal on an agreed upon date.

Funds - Funds are like mixing a bunch of stocks, bonds and other investments into a big bucket and investing in a few droplets of that concoction. Also known as Mutual Funds.

Retirement - The lingo and rules are so different between countries (example: a 401k in the USA usually refers to what is called RRSP's in Canada) so it's tough to get into details.

These types of investments are usually a 'tax deferment'. This means you won't be taxed on the amount you invest today, but instead, when you pull out the money at retirement. This helps to give you an income tax break now, build up a cushy retirement fund, and potentially pull out the cash at a lower tax rate later. One insider tip is to invest those tax returns you get at the end of the year after you submit your taxes. That money is actually the tax you saved by investing in your RRSP. When you withdraw funds from your RRSP in your retirement, you'll get taxed on that money but you will already be ahead of the game because you'll have invested your tax return decades earlier and shouldn't feel the burn of paying taxes.

I am not a financial guru, so obviously seek experienced advice on anything to do with investments. Duh.

THE NEW BUDGET

We need to make a new budget.
You have been faced with a ton of mind changing questions and future altering exercises. I would hypothesis that you are not the same person today as the person who started reading this book. You've made changes to your spending habits, started to pay off debt and save money on interest, sold off unused things and have even set up a savings plan.

That old budget you made back at the beginning might (SHOULD) look a little different.

Let's compare them to see where you have managed to lower your cost of living and save on interest.

WORKBOOK 14

Head back over to the original budget and see where you have already saved money and made changes.

Feel free to white out old numbers or jot your new numbers down on the page. At this point you have likely cancelled many services, lowered your debts from selling items online, etc. Your budget deserves to reflect this!

How much money have you saved already?

FUTURE Budget!

Now this is where it gets really fun! You know what your budget USED to look like, but you are putting some really fantastic changes into play here. I want you to make ONE more budget, and this time, **you are going to pretend its 1 year from now.**

Write out your budget like you have already cancelled as many services as possible, paid off as much debt as you think can actually happen by one year from now, and so on!

This budget will give you a snap shot of what your financial situation can look like if you just KEEP GOING along this amazing path!

Fill out your future budget sheet. What does your potential financial situation look like one year from now?

14 - When You Actually Need To Spend

Life costs money. We are all human beings who need things, occasionally want things and are going to end up shopping. I have outlined my best advice, tips and strategies for saving a ton of cash when you actually need to spend it!

Charge everything on credit cards

This is literally the opposite advice of every single 'get out of debt' guide you will ever read. They all tell you to promptly slice and dice your plastic into smithereens and use cash for every purchase from now on.
I think that is bat shit crazy.

You just want to be debt free, not teleport back to the 1850's. You need credit cards for virtually everything these days and I couldn't imagine living without one. The more I travel the more I see people not even accepting cash for purchases, so I really don't think cutting up your cards for good is a smart idea.

The advice to cut up the cards and use cash is given to people because they have demonstrated poor credit card habits in the past. I get that. Once I ate 2 entire boxes of mint chocolate Girl Guide cookies and demonstrated that I had really poor cookie eating habits. From that experience, I've actually learned how not to plow through junk food like a bull dozer therefore stopping myself from feeling embarrassingly ill. It doesn't mean I will never eat cookies again, it just means I got better at it through my mistakes.
Find the same lesson with your credit cards and you will be just fine.

My advice is to charge everything on your credit cards. **I mean everything.** Your groceries, your gas, even if you bought a $1 soda.

Here's why:

- Points. With the right credit card, you can get mountains of airline points, hotel points, or even cash back. When all of your purchases are going through the card, they are all counting towards your next trip. I have a TD Visa Infinite Privilege card and it gives me tons of Aeroplan miles (which I can use across all the Star Alliance partners) for simple everyday purchases.

- Tracking. It's really hard to see if you have improved your spending habits if you are only paying with cash and not collecting and tallying up receipts. Credit card statements are one of the best ways to keep track of spending month after month, and especially at tax time! Make sure you are diligently checking to see that the charges on your credit card were actually made by you (see Liability below).

- It's FREE. 99% of credit cards do not have a 'charge' to use it, so you are not racking up any fees by doing this. If you currently have a credit card that charges an annual fee, check to see if there is a no-fee option with that same provider. Once you tackle your debt, see if switching back to an annual fee card makes sense based on the number of purchases you are putting on that card.

- Liability. If someone steals your info and makes a crazy purchase on your credit card, your bank is the one who takes care of getting you off the hook. They are liable for the fraud charge, not you! In most cases they will refund the amount back onto your card instantly while they investigate the thief and deal with it behind the scenes. If someone takes your wallet of cash and goes and buys something, you have no control over it and an impending cry fest on your hands.

- Emergencies. I am NOT saying you should even think about racking these suckers back up with a balance, but hey, what if it was life or death? If you have a credit card (with its balance at ZERO of course) and a $10,000 limit, you have some breathing room in case of some imperative circumstance.

Here is the major caveat in *NEON LIGHTS*:

Pay if off right away.
Not tomorrow, not next week, **NOW**.
Transfer cash right onto the credit card the SECOND after you use it to pay before you even take your next breath of air. Now that you have paid off that debt you can bet your booty that you are not going to let it climb back up again.
When you pay it off the instant after you use it, you are not getting charged any interest. *YAY!*

I have an app on my phone where it's free to transfer cash to my credit card and it takes 2 seconds. Making this a die-hard habit will ensure you rack up the travel points and stay debt free like a mmmmffkkkkaaa!

WORKBOOK 15

Do you have a credit card that gives you travel points or cash back?
If you do, **see how many points you earned from your last 12 months of purchases** and what you can redeem those points for. Also, **estimate how many more points you would earn if you put every purchase on the card.** Does it equal flights for two to Paris? Or a big enough cash back check to buy them yourself?

Do you have an easy way (like an app) to put cash on your credit card after you make a purchase?
Check with your bank to see if they have an easy and free app to do this step for you.

Promo Codes

A promo code is a unique combination of letters or numbers that enter into a sales page at checkout to apply a discount to your online purchase. Don't checkout of an online store without finding a promo code. 95% of the time, no matter the type of shopping you are doing, a promotional code exists that will lower your total bill. I used to have to hunt these babies down by googling them, signing up to the brands newsletters in hopes they would email me one (and then immediately unsubscribing), or asking friends if they had one I could use.
Until now.
There is a chrome extension (which is like an app for the Chrome browser on your desktop) that does all the hunting for you. It's called Honey and its bloody brilliant!
When you head to any online shop, from Abercrombie to Zappos, Honey will automatically find all the promo codes that exist and apply them for you at checkout. It's free and has saved me tons of money on purchases I needed to make.
Remember: Honey is not an excuse to go shopping. I deactivate it when normally using my computer and ONLY activate it when I actually need to buy something, thereby stopping it from enticing me to shop when I don't need to. I highly suggest you only active Honey when you're really needing to find a discount on a particular item.

Airline Point Shopping Portals

Do you have an airline point's card like Airmiles, Aeroplan, Mileage Plus or Skymiles?
Well I sure hope you do. Airline point cards are free and allow you to rack up hundreds of miles you can exchange for free or upgraded flights. Winning!
Some people have a Visa or MasterCard that is also affiliated with a major airline point system. Other people just have a separate point's card that can be used when they shop in person at certain stores.
What a lot of people DON'T know is that each airline point system has its own online shopping portal that includes all the online stores you already shop at, letting you earn double and triple the miles.

For example, if you have an Aeroplan card, before you buy ANYTHING online, check if that store is located inside Aeroplan's own 'Estore' FIRST. Forever 21, Michael Kors, eBay, Sephora and Macy's are just a small sample of the stores that are listed. You enter in your Aeroplan number, click on the store you were already going to shop at anyway, and BOOM- You are now earning extra points towards flights that you never would have.

Here are some examples of Airlines and other travel point systems that have online shopping portals to double dip and earn extra points through:

- Aeromexico: Mall Premier
- Air Baltic: PINS e-shop
- Air Canada: Aeroplan eStore
- Air France: Flying Blue Shopping
- Alaska: Mileage Plan Shopping
- Alitalia: MilleMiglia Mall
- All Nippon Airways: ANA Mileage Mall
- American Airlines: AAdvantage eShopping
- British Airways: Gate 365
- Cathay Pacific: Asia Miles iShop
- Delta: Sky Miles Shopping
- e-Miles: e-Miles Market
- Etihad: Etihad Guest Earn Mall
- Finnair Plus: Finnair Plus Shop
- Hawaiian Airlines: HawaiianMiles Online Mall
- Japan Airlines: JAL Shopping Americas
- JetBlue: ShopTrue
- KLM: Shop at KLM
- Qantas: Qantas Shop
- Singapore Airlines: Krisshop
- Southwest: Rapid Rewards Shopping
- United: MileagePlus Shopping
- US Airways: Divident Miles Shopping Mall

Again, just like with the Honey extension DO NOT use these point systems as an excuse to shop.

When I absolutely need something, like ink for my printer or replacing a personal item I have used up, I just USE this portal instead of going to the stores website directly.
Why not, right!? It costs nothing and allows you to earn airline points on virtually everything you would ever need to purchase.
Don't browse these sites, just go on them when you already know the item you need to buy and leverage the free points.

Consider Used

Depending on the type of item you find yourself needing, ask yourself "would pre-owned or slightly used do the trick?"
Local Facebook buy/sell groups, Facebook marketplace, eBay, consignment shops, thrift stores and other online or in person businesses are great places to score deals.
My brother in law Mats, is a pretty frugal guy and is super mindful of what he spends his money on. He is the type of guy who reads the flyers, waits for things to go on sale and would rather go without than overpay for something. His best kept secret for getting some wild deals on unique and quality used items is at his local auction.

Another great way to get a good deal on something used is to ask around your circle of friends. What if you really needed to buy a lawnmower and your buddy has one he needed to sell. You get a great deal, he gets cash in his pocket instead of you giving it to a big box store. Win/win.

DIY

Another chapter in my 'things I learn from my brother in law' book, DIY. This guy built his own lake side TIKI bar for next to nothing, (which I am happy to be a summer patron of!)
Even though Mats is super handy and has the skill and knowledge to make something out of nothing, all levels can ride the DIY wave. There is a massive premium put onto products that are already assembled and more 'convenient' for the end consumer.

With a little imagination, you can make almost any product yourself for a fraction of what a store charges. Everything from headboards, to garden planters, to desk organizers. Big projects and little projects. Pinterest is the go-to for all things DIY!

High end brands -vs- 'no name' brands

Is it better to bargain shop for the no name brands with the lowest price tags?

A mistake I have made in the past was thinking that low end bargain brands (in clothing, household items, even food) would end up saving me money over time.
This was a major error that actually cost me more money in the long run.

Let's say I bought a jacket at Walmart that was a look alike to a major luxury brand at 1/10th of the price. Sounds like a steal of a deal right? Well, the price has to be paid somewhere.
After about 8-10 wears that jacket is likely pilling, the thin lining on the inside pockets have tattered holes, a button falls off, and I need to replace that coat before the season is over. Even if that jacket was $50, I will likely keep buying them over and over as they don't last at all.
If instead, I bought the luxury brand in a timeless style (example, my beige Burberry trench coat) I can wear it for years. It's not uncommon for a jacket like that to last a decade or more.
So what is better? Buying 20 cheap jackets over 10 years, or 1 quality jacket.
I vote quality.
When we buy 20 cheap jackets over a decade, we are continuing to fuel the demand for low end, low quality goods. Plus that is 20 times you wasted going shopping, 20 times you were tempted to buy other things, 20 times you could have been doing something more productive.
Speaking of my Burberry trench coat, it has been a staple in my daily wardrobe as I've been touring the UK this fall. I purchased it over 6 years ago and it still looks brand new, and even better, it's still in style.

If a brand new, high quality item is not in your budget, consider buying one used. Most luxury consignment stores have extremely strict valuations of condition for reselling second hand items and you can score a sweet deal. I purchased a Gucci top that was retail $600 for only $75 on an online consignment store and it looked brand freaking new. I couldn't even tell it was used. I've owned and worn that shirt for almost a decade and it still looks great.

Quality over quantity

There are a few items that I will shell out some major cash for, but they replace the need to buy countless cheaper items instead.

Diamond Studs. Round, dainty, white gold setting. I have worn these earrings almost every day for 8 years. They never go out of style and they go with absolutely everything. I don't feel tempted to buy the $15 cheap earrings you see in stands all over shops because they really aren't in the same league as my studs. I have probably saved thousands of dollars from not buying $20 here and $80 there of other fashion jewelry.

Jeans. I have no issue spending $300 on ONE pair of jeans if they fit me like a glove, are comfortable and I can wear them in a variety of different settings. I will keep them forever and it stops me from compulsively buying 'just okay' jeans.

Shoes I walk far distances in. No skimping here. Being a full time traveler I don't have room to pack 20 pairs of cute shoes. I need 1 or 2 pairs of comfortable, stylish, durable, quality shoes. I have some favourite brands, but I'm open to anything that allows me to walk thousands of steps a day without limping home.

Plastic Wrap & TP. LOL! I had to put these in here. No name plastic wrap doesn't cling to anything, ever. It's a total joke and a waste of money. Same goes with bargain TP, wow is that stuff coarse!

Things I will buy the cheap-o version of:

ANY trend clothing or jewelry. If something is a super-hot trend, here today gone tomorrow kind of vibe, I will go cheap on it. There is no point in buying any brand names or quality items here because it has a very short shelf life. Anything super bright, abstract, out there, trendy, or fashion forward can be picked up for under $20. Then I don't really care about donating or even selling it later on. I keep these items to a minimum of course, but it allows me the freedom to spice it up once in a while.
Costume jewelry is a great example of this.

'No name' pharmacy and store brands. Have you ever had a cold, went to go get some medication and you saw the big WALL of options. The brand name cold pills might be $17 and the no name brand beside it (with exactly the same ingredients) are $5, but you think somehow in your mind the trusted brand is going to get you feeling better faster? It won't. They are the same. Most 'no name' health and beauty products are 100% identical. This includes face wipes, shampoos, body wash, cold pills… really anything you can buy at a pharmacy. Read the ingredients and compare it for yourself, you will be blown away!

Handbags. Okay, maybe not the 'cheapest' kind of handbags out there for $20, but I am sure as heck not going to spend $4000 on one. That's INSANE. What is even more insane is when people buy a $4000 or even a $2000 handbag when they have debt on their credit cards. I have heard the phrase "a luxury handbag is an investment". No it's not. Every other girl and her dog has the same handbag. Millions of them have been made and sold and there is nothing unique or rare about them. Sure you can sell it second hand for about 1/2 of what you paid for it if it's in PRISTINE condition, but that doesn't always happen.
I find a mid-range bag, quality, maybe $100-$200 with no brands or logos all over them is the best way to go. They last a long time, look super stylish, usually have cool features like RFID security (more on that later) and won't leave me broke.

Lists

Go to the store with a list and a plan. Stick to it. Before you even leave your front door, have a clear and concise plan of what you NEED and where it might be located in the store. This way you can put on your blinders and head directly for what you came for. Trevor likes to approach any type of shopping like a 'Mission Impossible' directive. He looks over his game plan in the car, walks into the store with purpose, focuses on his target, and is OUT of there before anyone even knew he was there. I am not as hardcore as that, but I know when I have a list and a plan I am much more likely to thwart temptation.

Negotiate

It's not just for the markets in Marakesh. Albeit you probably won't get very far trying to negotiate for a top in Forever 21, you can still try out your bartering skills in many other situations.
On a larger scale, here are big ticket items you should always negotiate on, no exceptions: A house, a car, furniture, appliances, renovations, interest rates, rent, cable or phone bill, insurance premiums, extended warranties, electronics, website design, legal bills, and jewelry.
Even everyday transactions can be negotiated, especially if you're a regular, like: meal prep, dry cleaning, high end department stores, housekeeping and freelance services.

Trade & Swap

Let's say you have a friend who is a wonderfully talented hairdresser *(Hi, Lauren Steele!)* and you are in dire need of a dye job. Maybe you have something that Lauren, I mean your hairdresser, needs, like web design. If she was going to hire someone anyway, and you were going to pay some salon anyway, why don't you hook up and do a service swap? You both save money and get what you want in the end! Plus it's a really great excuse to get together, support each other, and obviously drink wine. *(Call me, Lauren!)*

15 - Budget Hacks

I am all about a good life HACK.
Even better when that hack means I can travel more ;)
I know that you and I will have different budgets and different travel goals, but I found 3 budget hacks that will make your life much easier!

#1 Start with the END GAME

In April 2015 I was drooling over the 'end game' of being able to spend 6 months in Ecuador.
Woah... REALITY CHECK right?!... how the HECK are you going to afford this Kashlee??
By researching what my end game really costs!
I looked up things like: When the cheapest time to visit is, the cost of actual accommodations that were available during my travel dates, food prices, flights, etc.
This gave me a 'total' amount that I could work with. If I don't know what I am dealing with, it will forever stay a dream!
Without researching it, I would never have known if it was possible or not!
TIP: Know what you want, by what date. Know exactly where you want to go. Don't be vague. Research it to get all the info and costs you will need. The hotel or rental, your transportation, everything.

#2 Reverse Engineer that shizzz

Once I had done my entire savvy internet sleuthing, it was time to make a reverse engineered budget. I added up the total cost of living budget for the full 6 months.
Now with a total I had something to work with! I knew I had to make/save 'x' amount of money by Oct 1 2015.

By eliminating a 'cost of living' at home, saving extra cash and researching all affordable places, Ecuador beach front living was actually CHEAPER than my life at home!

TIP: Lower your cost of living at home and use the extra budget towards your trip! See where you can save on NOW that will add up to what you need for your end game goal.

- Sell a bunch of old clothes, shoes, handbags, throw pillows, whatever you aren't using!
- Look at your credit card statement and see how much money you will save by cancelling things like cable, subscription boxes, music services, etc, from now until your deadline. (For me it was over $2000!)
- If you want to go on a long trip, sublease or rent out your place to at least cover those costs.
- After trying all these tips, see what amount is left between your end game goal, and the funds you now have. Take the total difference, divide it by your deadline date and find a way to SAVE that amount each month. You can take a % off what you make, or save what you would have spent on wine, nails, dining, shopping, etc.

#3 Rinse and Repeat!

Once you have reached your end game goal, TAKE THAT TRIP and enjoy every minute of it. When you get back home, start planning the next one :)
It will keep you from compulsively shopping and make you more mindful of where your money is spent!
TIP: If you always have a life experience goal with a deadline, you will waste less money on crap.

By the way....
This kind of budget hack can be applied to anything! Buying a car, saving up for school, really any big purchase you want to be strategic with. Simply apply this template and it's a one size fits all for any goal.

WORKBOOK 16

Identify a goal you want to make a reality.
Use the reverse engineering template to work out how much you will need to save each month to make it happen. Attach an 'end date' you want to have the goal accomplished by.

Part Five

EARN

16 - That Entrepreneur Life

Let's talk about making money, because without a good steady income, traveling the globe wouldn't be possible. Running my own business is what allows me to come and go as I please, without having to worry about going broke and having to return home with my tail between my legs. Having a career is fundamental in having a happy and balanced life.

While we are on this topic, if you ever see any literature about 'quit your job and travel the world' and it doesn't mention needing to grow your own business, toss it aside. It's such a load of crap for someone to claim you can simply quit working and just vacation for the rest of your life. You can't. Unless you inherit a fortune, win the lottery, or sell a start-up for millions of dollars, you will have to fund your lifestyle the good ol' fashioned way, working your butt off!
I work full time hours (or more) while I am traveling, even if from the outside it looks like I am living a more relaxed lifestyle. By combining my hobbies, passions and work together, I am able to have the feeling of not working, even if I am hustling overtime.

I never thought I would be a full time traveler and a digital nomad. Well, wait a sec…that's kind of a lie. I KNEW deep inside my soul that I was not meant for a cubical. I also knew, with the influence and exposure to my crazy entrepreneurial parents that I would eventually run my own business. I guess what I didn't know, was how soon I could actually make it happen and how it would turn out to be my DREAM JOB.

What I do:

Travel Blogger
I came, I saw, I conquered, and I posted it on the 'Gram. I get paid to travel to different cities all over the world and blog/post about my adventures. I love being able to share my journey, teaching others about different cultures and destinations across the globe.

Writer
I put on my writers hat more often these days than ever before. I write content about attractions, hotels, cities, travel hacks and life tips. I also write for other websites and publications on my areas of expertise. And of course, writing this book, which I hope to be one of many! The moment I realized I could help people with my writing, I knew I had to make it a big part of my life.

Mentor
Business development is my jam. If people ask me what my hobbies are, my first response is always "BUSINESS!" I'm extremely passionate about helping entrepreneurs find their niche, brand, purpose and place in the business world; everything from websites, to social media, to building an audience. It's so rewarding helping someone grow into a profitable career that they have always dreamed of!

Host
Last but not least, my newest title, 'Podcast Host'! At the time of writing this book, I am just putting the final touches on my upcoming podcast "The High Maintenance Minimalist" which gives me butterflies just thinking about! It's an extension of this book, giving you a weekly dose of travel and 'living with less' inspiration. I've got some sensational guests lined up and I'm looking forward to interviewing and learning from them!

Let me be the first to tell you, I did not head towards my career with everything planned out from the start. What I do now has evolved from a decade of trial and error, making mistakes, having success (and failures) and finding my way. I've taken many wrong turns, but they all gifted me something in return.

Growing up as the youngest child in a family of serial entrepreneurs, I was an early adopter to the philosophy of blazing my own trail and doing things differently. I watched my parents grow multiple businesses from the ground up and it showed me that anything was possible if I put a little hustle into it.

I remember my first business, back in 5th grade, selling coveted information. I leveraged the mountain of Seventeen magazines my older sister had in the house by copying out 'fan mail' addresses for celebrities, and making a booklet of them on my DOS computer. (Wait, can we just pause for a second! Yes, teen magazines used to put out one or two fan mail addresses a month for people like Luke Perry, SWOON. Crazy right!)

I took these booklets and sold them at school for $1 a piece! It was good information at the time since the internet was brand new and 'Googling it' didn't yet exist.

I had multiple projects on the go throughout all of elementary; including a popcorn stand and designing mesh drawstring bags.

In high school I helped design, stock, set up and operate a clothing store with my best guy friend Shane, all while juggling classes, which to be honest didn't go so well. When we would take buying trips into downtown Toronto to pick out new labels and pieces for upcoming seasons, it hardly made me want to sit my ass back down in a classroom. I became totally restless, uninterested and completely bored with everything to do with school, which was a total 180 for me, because I had always been an overachiever with top grades. I dropped out of my last semester of high school with only a few months to go to graduation.

I moved downtown for a while and dabbled in some sales jobs, but ended up giving up my High Park apartment to take a once in a lifetime opportunity to live and work in Mexico. My sister Becky got a job at a resort in Huatulco and was begging me to apply to come down and work with her.

They were looking for people who could act/dance in the nightly shows and host activities, like water aerobics, at the main pool during the day. While I didn't have any sports skills whatsoever, acting and dancing was something I knew I could 'fake it till I make it' and learn how to master as I went. With a basic grasp of high school level Spanish, an adventurous personality, and a big smile, I made it through the interview and was put on a plane to Mexico at 18 years old.

It was the best and the worst time of my life. The best parts were the freedom, adventure, limelight, attention, and the exotic new lifestyle that was now mine! I learned how to speak much better Spanish, dance and act in the shows, and eventually even how to instruct a water aerobics class. One of my main jobs during the day was to organize the costumes and outfits for the nightly shows, which was insanely stressful because one mistake could cost the show. As dancers, we had only a few seconds to complete a costume change, and if everything wasn't exactly in the order it should be, meant throwing the whole next scene into disorganized chaos. Other than the pressure to do everything right and be 'on' all the time, it was one of the most fun jobs I've ever had. We got to live in the hotel just like a guest, complete with housekeeping, eating meals at the restaurants, even dancing at the bar and disco. In fact, part of our actual job WAS to drink, socialize and have fun in the bar with the guests. At 18, all of this attention and 'fame' I felt was great for getting me out of my shell, but was horrible for my wellbeing long term.

I began to drink too much, staying up way too late, and started skipping the daily 6am dance practice the next morning. It got to a level where I had to take two shots of vodka before each water aerobics class at noon, which was a terribly unprofessional and unhealthy habit. I was self-medicating with alcohol because the lifestyle at such a young age had gone to my head, but also because I wanted to drown out my surroundings. The resort I worked at had some major sexual harassment issues. Not only were we highly encouraged to flirt and be cute with the guests, but it seemed that the male employees had the same directive with us.

My sister and I, along with another Canadian girl who worked with us at the hotel, were constantly being harassed every hour of the day.

Late night phone calls, guys drunkenly banging on our doors, groping us at the pool or at dance practice, even trying to force themselves on us on many occasions; all to which our boss would reply with something like "Well this is what you do to men! It's not their fault you are beautiful women. This is life!"

Yeah, Stone Age shit, right?

One day, I'd had enough. I quietly packed my bags, called a cab, and left the resort. I ended up taking a 12 hour bus to the neighboring state of Chiapas and worked there as a freelance model for a while. That was, until I got deported, which will have to be another story for another book!

Coming back home to Canada at 20 years of age left me eager to start the next chapter of my life. I soon left Ontario for a place I had never been to before, Saskatchewan. *(You know, the flat place you can watch your dog run away for days)*

SK had something I wanted, cheap real estate. My brother Cody and I found a house in a small town called Melville for $20k. Coming from the Toronto area in Ontario, this kind of housing price was UNHEARD OF, as parking spots cost more than that!

When we sold the same property for $68k only 6 months later, I knew Real Estate investing would be a big part of my life. Timing was everything in Saskatchewan during those years. The real estate industry in SK had never had a boom like other provinces, yet it had tons of resources and jobs. As more and more eyes set their gaze to the prairies, I knew I needed to act quickly if I wanted to take further advantage of this market.

I knew working in the car industry was a great way to make money, so that would be my next endeavour.

My father sold RV's and even owned his own car dealership when I was younger and I always had an interest in following suit. My oldest brother Chris was even running a large dealership in Vancouver, so I used him as a resource in becoming successful myself.

I started at the bottom, approaching people as they came to browse on the lot, and worked my way up to internet sales manager and eventually a finance manager for one of the largest dealerships in the province. All the while I was taking Psych classes at the U of R to further the education that I had tossed aside as a teenager.

The income allowed me to buy and sell a few more properties and invest what was left over. I felt like I had 'made it'.

Being a finance manager was my dream job for so many years, but even at the height of that success I still felt something was missing. Despite the great pay, I was still working in an office building, at someone else's business instead of my own. I remember not even being allowed to take a vacation that I had earned, and since I have major wanderlust, that kind of life wasn't going to fly with me. Since I had been successful in my own real estate investments and I basically studied the market daily as a hobby, real estate looked to be the answer.

I passed the exams, got my real estate license and started building up a name for myself in the Regina area. Again, timing seemed to be everything as the real estate in Regina literally started to BOOM like never before. I constantly listed houses that resulted in buyers entering bidding wars within days of going on the market. Jobs were paying more than ever and young couples had significant income to purchase homes that were still considered very underpriced compared to other Canadian cities. Between my own listings, buyers and a new contract I had with a home builder, I took on a partner to help with the work load. We ended up bonding and taking our real estate careers to the next level together…. That was until… well my meltdown! That hot, fast life had created more problems than good, and it was just a matter of time until I fell down hard. I had piled too much on my plate and trying to maintain that lifestyle had become impossible. I was hosting events, filming a TV show, running a demanding real estate business alongside managing new home builds, not to mention all the financial pressure I had put on myself like a brand new house, 2 luxury cars, etc. I was making killer money, but my lifestyle was sucking it out faster than I could make it. I was already working 16 hour days, what else could I do? Hence the breakdown.

Right around the same time as my downward spiral into rock bottom, the real estate market dried right up in the city. What goes up must come down, right? Nothing (and nobody) is meant to stay on top forever.

After getting a taste of what most people would call extreme success, and the taste of being my own boss, I knew that anything I did afterwards would have to be on my OWN terms.

I needed to create a career using my passions, skills and interests that wasn't dependent on swinging markets or what other people wanted. Something I create and control.

A job where I could have the freedom to be myself.

That is where I am today. Happier, wiser and finally figuring it out after a decade of trial and error.

My true loves are business development, influence, writing, traveling, and building relationships. In the past my jobs might have had traveling, or perhaps business development, but none of them were able to combine all my passions into one.

Until now!

I do realize how instrumental each piece was in the puzzle that is now my life but it sure took a lot to get there. Each job I've had and each mistake I've made has given me a blueprint and template to navigate the world with. Each wrong turn has shown me the right way to go. Each job I tried but didn't stick with, has taught me a set of skills I needed for the future. Gone are the days where you get a job right out of school and stay there until the day you retire.

The clothing store taught me responsibility and how retail operation work. The resort taught me awareness, listening to my gut and being more extroverted. Starting at the bottom in the car sales world taught me drive, ambition and the power of persuasion. Being a finance manager taught me about interest, loans, money management and the inner workings of the financial world. Real estate taught me importance of timing, market patterns, what hard work really looks like, and how capable I really am.

Looking back at my work history, I'm proud to have tried new things, even if they didn't always work out. Nothing ventured, nothing gained. No risk, no reward.

Had I not taken any of those steps, I would not be where I am today. *Eat your heart out world!*

There is no right or wrong way to approach your career, education, or life in general.

Nobody has it all figured out on the first attempt.

My purpose in telling you all of my working background is to inspire you to TRY whatever it is you want to pursue. Even if it results in a dead end, I promise you will come out with a new perspective and wisdom needed to advance to the next level of your life.

By sitting still, you could be missing out on the events and moments that will ultimately shape the rest of your life.
Make that mistake.
Try and fail.
It's only going to add character and experience to the person you are now.

If you feel the same emptiness that I felt in my career, consider what else you can do for a living that will motivate and inspire you! There are no rules here!
You might want to take on a second job, a part time project, or shift your full time career to a different industry.
Whatever aligns best with your goals and your passions - do it!

It's never to late to start something new. I look at my parents who are currently living in Nova Scotia and running not one, but two art galleries, at almost 70 years old. My dad re-discovered his love for painting later on in life and wasn't going to let anything stop him from creating a legacy around it. Did they know how to open a gallery? No. But they did it anyway, and it's been a smashing success!
There is one thing I know for sure, and that is they will never feel the sting of regret of not taking action on something they're passionate about. Watching how much enthusiasm and energy they have makes me realize how important it is to keep following your heart!

17 - Your Dream Job

Secondary stream of income

Nothing says 'pack yo bags!' like an extra paycheck!
Being self-employed is one of the most freeing, exciting, scream at the top of your lungs frustrating, yet rewarding things in the world.
Even if you have a career working for the man that you never intend to quit, this section is just as vital to you as it is for someone looking to be a digital nomad.

No matter what industry you're in or company you work for, nothing in life is certain but death and taxes. The recession of 2008 showed us that no financial power or Wall Street mega corporation is safe. Neither are the little guys.

Having more than ONE income stream is very important for securing your future, maximizing the amount of money you can earn and having extra freedom to see the world.

Raise your hand in the air, like you just don't care, if you want to:

- ✓ Have a second stream of income
- ✓ Learn how to start your own business
- ✓ Make money while traveling
- ✓ Set up a passive or residual income stream
- ✓ Turn your passions into profits

Even the smallest amount of extra income can make a tremendous difference in your life.

If you were able to make even $80 a WEEK doing something on the side, that would be $4,160 a year!

$4,160 extra per year could give you (ANNUALLY!):
- An all-inclusive trip to the Dominican Republic
- A 2 month stay in Thailand
- One week in a swanky New York City hotel for New Year's Eve
- **OR $119,829.26, in total savings over 20 years** *earning a modest 3% interest.*

There are a few different paths you can go down!

1. The Traditional route. Working for a company in a specific location.

2. Jobs that are moderately location independent, working for someone else.

3. Jobs that are moderately location independent, working for self.

4. Jobs that are 100% location independent, working for someone else.

5. Jobs that are 100% location independent, working for self.

1.The traditional route

If you are more of a conservative, low risk kind of person a secondary part time job in a more traditional sense might be up your alley. Before applying for any second job, map out your availability, flexibility and limitations so you are not biting off more than you can chew.

Here are some examples of in person, brick and mortar type jobs that you could apply for on a part time basis. You can look for these on local job boards, job sites, even local Facebook groups.

Minimal skill or experience needed:

Uber Driver
Dog Walker
Babysitter

Paper Route
Waitress
Hostess
Barista
Retail Sales Clerk
School Bus Driver
Customer Service
Catering Staff
Cashier
Cleaner
Receptionist
Personal Assistant
Errand Runner
Fruit Picker
Food Delivery

Medium to High amount of skill or experience:

Bank Teller
Admin Assistant
Tour Guide
Lifeguard
Referee
Personal Trainer
Mechanic
Make Up Artist
Tutor
Hair Stylist
Travel Agent
Massage Therapist
Accountant
Bookkeeper
House Painter
Security Guard
Construction
Aesthetician

All of these jobs would likely be working under a company that paid you by the hour or a pre-negotiated rate. The benefit of a traditional type part time job is that you will be paid for the hours you put in, compared to the uncertainty of starting your own business. The drawbacks are: less control over hours, less flexibility for travel, less creative control, building someone else's brand and business for them. If your intentions are to build something you are truly passionate about (and will allow you to travel) then a traditional second job might hold you back.

Working online or running your own online business is hands down the BEST way to make extra cash to travel and to finance your travels WHILE you are actually abroad.
Right from the horse's mouth, growing and running your own biz is by NO means easy, but worth every sacrifice in the long run.

2. Jobs Abroad that are moderately location independent, Working for others:

These abroad positions usually require you to commit to a location or a certain area (aka- It's half freedom based, half real world based). They can however be done abroad and usually involve a lot of travel, so they are still very relevant to a business minded nomad.

Just like the online company jobs, these positions will usually be held under an already established company, with you as the employee. Some might be seasonal, part time, full time or temporary, but they all involve a travel based lifestyle. They commonly need your commitment to stay in one place for some time, but that place is usually abroad, and sometimes you get to choose where!

Cruise Ships/Yachts
Hotels, Restaurants & Bars (chef)
Travel Nurse
Nanny/Au Pair

Farm Help/Fruit Picking
Film/Entertainment (stage hand, stage performer, film extra)
Festival Worker/Event Coordinator
Language Teacher
Flight Attendant/Pilot

3. Jobs that are Moderately Location Independent- Working for Self:

These jobs might need you to commit to a location for a certain amount of time, but you can be your own boss!

• *Artist*
Unless you are selling digital prints online, you might need to pick a location to work out of to grow your popularity for a while. Whether it's painting, sculpting or another art form, this is a very creative way to earn a living and focus on your passions. You could pick any city worldwide that has a vibrant art scene to work from!

• *Festival Vendor/Crafts*
If you make your own crafts or jewelry you have many opportunities to make an income at markets and festivals. You could travel to different cities each weekend, or stay in one area seasonally to promote and sell your creations.

• *House Sitter or Pet Sitter*
There is a growing need for house sitters and pet sitters all over the world. Many membership sites will link up a person in need of help and an experienced house sitter together.
There are opportunities available all over the world that range from a few days, to a year or longer. Some people just need help with keeping the house plants alive, while others are looking for sitters with special skills, like taking care of horses.

Mix of Jobs Abroad that are moderately location independent: Working for others & working for self:

Here are a group of job opportunities that might be done with a company, but could also become your own company, depending on your drive and skill level! You can decide whether to go at it alone, or work under a boss instead.

•*Vacation Home Manager*
Thanks to the internet, renting out your property as a vacation rental is a very popular thing to do. But what about making sure it's cleaned, fully stocked, in working order, etc. Many owners with just 1 listing aren't looking to get a full time property manager, but still need help. You could make your own business of cleaning, stocking, and helping new arrivals at independent vacation rental homes anywhere in the world. On the flip side, you could also seek employment with an abroad property management company.

•*Tour Guide*
Have you ever been somewhere you loved so much you just wanted to stay forever? Well, if you became a freelance tour guide in that city, you could! This is a great idea for an expat who is super knowledgeable about a city or certain area and is a people person. If you don't like winging it on your own, you could always apply with an existing tour company in your country of choice.

•*Ski/Scuba/Yoga/Fitness/Adventure Instructor*
Travel and vacations mean activities! If you are great at water sports, yoga, climbing, hiking, or other adventurous things, you can always start your own instructor company.
Working for yourself you can pick the locations, your hours, rate of pay and have total control over your brand. If you would rather utilize someone else's hard work, you can always apply to a company that is looking to hire.

- **Hair Dresser/Beauty/Nails/Massage**

No matter what country you are in worldwide, beauty services are always being offered. You can either start up your own salon, or apply to work in an existing salon all over the world. Obtaining and keeping clientele usually means staying in one place for a while, but that doesn't mean that place has to be at home!

- **Event Planner/Destination Wedding Planner**

I have a friend who moved to Mexico to work with hotels as a destination wedding planner. She started her own business, but there are also opportunities to work with established companies worldwide.

4. Jobs that are 100% location independent, working for someone else

Here is where the real freedom starts: finding a job or career that you can do from ANYWHERE, even if it's for a brand, company or employer!

Are online jobs for actual companies real?
Absolutely! Huge companies like Disney, Amazon, Dell, and United Airlines are just a handful of forward thinking super powers that hire location independent employees.
This saves them a ton of money in expensive office costs and allows them to hire people based on their relevant skills instead of their location. They might set your hours and rate of pay, but you will also have clear tasks and workloads. If the idea of taking the full leap into being your own boss makes you dizzy, these are likely up your alley.

Here are some examples:

Data Entry
Customer Service and Customer Support Representative
Online Language Teacher

I have heard of many successful cases of an individual approaching their boss to negotiate a remote location position or contract. If your current job doesn't require you to actually BE in an office, give it a try! As long as you are equally productive and there is no risk for the company, you might have a good shot at it!

5. Jobs that are 100% location independent, working for self

The following section is going to cover types of jobs that allow total freedom, meaning jobs you can do from anywhere in the world and will allow you to move and travel as you please.

Another word that is being used to describe a person who works in a location independent based industry is a DIGITAL NOMAD. Digital nomads are people who leverage the online world to work in whatever city or country they please. They usually move around a lot and like to mix travel and business together.
Here is the list of jobs where you will run the show yourself.
You will be 100% self-employed working as a freelancer and an entrepreneur, building your business the way you see fit. The master of your own universe! They always have the highest earning potential (cha-ching!) but take time, blood, sweat and tears to grow.

This is full digital nomad status at its finest, and in my opinion, the BEST way to go!

•Writing
Companies, blogs, magazines and other publications are always looking for strong writers.
The average writer can expect to earn anywhere from $0.15 to $0.90 per word.
For example, if you got paid even $0.20 per word on a 1200 word article, only 4 times a month, that would be close to $1000/m in earnings.

- *Blogging*

Individuals with a large following or a niche market can earn a living by blogging. While it's not instant income and can take anywhere from 6 months to 2 years to turn a profit, blogging is a great way to build your own brand, voice and business.

Money is earned by selling advertising space, affiliate links, copywriting, sponsorships, and more.

- *Resume Writer*

Many people are clueless about writing their own resume and when the need all of a sudden arises for one, they need help from a pro. If you are great with grammar, spelling, writing, etc and you have hiring experience, you might want to look into becoming a resume coach. A basic resume might go for $50-$70, with a detailed and extremely competitive resume landing you approx. $250.

- *Transcription*

So much of our visual and digital world requires transcription at some point. Meaning typed out word for word. This job is great for people who type fast, listen well and have a lot of patience for repetition. You can expect to charge anywhere from $0.75 to $2.50 per audio minute.

- *Affiliate Marketer*

This job goes well with blogging, but doesn't require a blog in order to have success. An affiliate marketer will promote and sell other companies products in exchange for a percentage of the sale. It's great because the original company will take care of shipping, invoicing, inventory, etc. Your role would be only to refer prospects to purchase the item. There is no 'average' amount for an AM, as it can range from mere cents a year to hundreds of thousands of dollars.

- *Online Course Creator/Instructor*

Being proficient in a certain area or having an experienced knowledge on a topic can translate into a great income. There are millions of things people are looking to learn online, so the sky is the limit on this one.

You could create courses on topics like (but not limited to): social media, writing a book, yoga training, calligraphy, astrology, learning a language, building a website, botany… literally anything.

•Membership Site Creator/Owner
Membership sites are great for businesses that revolve around something that is always updating and has new information to offer. A great example of this would be creating a membership site where people pay $9 a month and they get access to all the flight and hotel deals you find. The topics and niche possibilities of a membership site are unlimited.

•E-store/Drop Shipping
More than ever before, consumers are shopping online instead of in stores. If you have a product that you made yourself, or even one you have sourced, having an online e-store is a great way to capitalize on global sales. This can be as big or small as you want it to be, like a full time online clothing store, or just selling wedding invitations on Etsy. Drop shipping is when you don't ever physically create or see the product yourself and rely on larger manufacturers to make and ship the product to your buyers.

•Social Influencer
This is a very new way to make income online, but has always existed in some form in the past. Brands will pay a person with a large following to talk about, wear, use, or promote one of their products on social media. Good social influencers will only choose to work with brands they would actually use themselves and companies that align with their core values.
I work as a social influencer and I love being able to partner with brands and products I truly believe in. In a world where we are all bombarded with commercials and ads from big brands, it's nice to have smaller companies and individuals working together to offer real value.

•Stock Investor or Day Trader
This avenue can be a scary one to go down, but extremely profitable. If you have a high risk tolerance and you love to play the stock market, this job might be for you!
Not something to consider if you have no experience in the industry.

•Video Editor

I suck at editing videos, but some people are great at it and have a huge opportunity to make income with their skills. Video editing is needed by the biggest companies out there, right down to the local food blogger. It's become a major need in our digital world! You can expect to charge anywhere from $15-$40 an hour for quality work. Experts can charge a LOT more!

•Voice Over Artist

I personally loved being a voice over artist. For me it was fun to try out for different jobs and lend my voice to a variety of projects! I did everything from safety videos, to jewelry commercials, to phone directory recordings. For this you need to be able to read very well out loud, have a quiet recording space and a great microphone. I would make around $100 for a short 15 second job, $300-$500 for a 30 second commercial, $500-$1000+ for a longer video reading, EBook, or larger job.

•Photographer

There are many different types of photography you can get into if you have the eye for it: wedding, engagement, portrait, real estate, newborn, travel, etc! An average photographer can expect to charge around $25-$75/h, semi pro $50-$150/h, professional $75-$250/h and top professional $500+/h.

My life long friend Victoria, and photographer for the cover art of this book, is the perfect example of running a photography biz. She sets her own hours, hand picks the locations and clients she wants to work with, and gets to travel the world! It didn't start out that way, but her hustle, drive and passion blossomed into a fun and vibrant career.

•Online Fitness Instructor/Health Coach

Fitness has entered the online world in a big way. Many clients can't or don't want to enter crowded gyms and would rather do their workouts at home. Online fitness instructors are becoming more popular with Skype training sessions, recording workout videos, and even running online boot camps.

My husband Trevor has made a career doing this for the last 5 years.

He used to train in person, but his income was restricted to the amount of hours there were in the day and how many people he could fit into the room. Moving his business online allowed him to help more people than ever.

Online health coaches are also growing in popularity. You can have virtual clients for things like: meal prep help, nutrition, meditation, naturopathy, competitive sport, stress relief, etc.

•*Online Tutor*

If you want to take your teaching skills online, being a virtual tutor is a great way to help others and make an income. If you are just super knowledgeable on a particular topic (but not formally educated on it) you can expect to earn $15-$25/h. If you are educated and highly experienced the hourly rate can very between $30-$80/h.

•*Business Coach or Finance Coach*

If you have successfully launched, operated or helped grow a business, you will have skills and insight you can charge for. New entrepreneurs are always needing guidance on starting a business, growing a business, social media, marketing, branding, communication, leadership, finances and more.

MIX of Jobs that are 100% location independent: working for others and working for self.

There are pros and cons for working online for a company or just going at it solo. These next location independent job examples can either be found working under a company as an employee, or running your own business as a self-employed entrepreneur. You would make that choice.

•*Sales Rep*

If you have the gift of persuasion you could start your own sales company online, or work remotely for an existing company. As long as you only need Wi-Fi to do your job, you are good to go to any country that has a Wi-Fi connection.

- ***Book Keeper***
With prior bookkeeping experience you can freelance for work using online sites, which will allow you total control and flexibility. On the other hand, you could also work remotely for a bookkeeping company that sends you work on a flat rate or hourly basis.

- ***Virtual Assistant***
There are companies that will connect you with business people needing an assistant, or you can just use the business skills you have and find the clients yourself! Companies will take a percentage of your wage, but either way, being a VA is a great way to work from anywhere.

- ***Web Designer/Graphic Designer***
I don't see the need for a good web designer going away anytime soon! Individuals and businesses need websites, like, yesterday! You could either work for a design firm or go solo and approach small businesses yourself. Either option is still a wonderful way to earn money while traveling.

- ***Web or App Coder/Developer***
It takes big brains to enter into this career, but it comes with big payoffs as well! The earning potential is unlimited when you can code and develop for large complex projects. You might be stuck behind a computer most of the day, but that computer could be oceanfront in Thailand.

- ***Translator***
A translator job might mean in person, or even online. There is a growing need for translator guides on tourism trips, as well as online translation for copywriting, audio and video. There are firms you can connect with, or simply advertise yourself as a freelancer.

- ***Social Media Manager/Marketing Manager***
Many companies and entrepreneurs are too swamped to run their own social media channels or properly market their brands. If you have experience in either of these you can earn a full time income on the go.

What about MLM (Multi-Level Marketing) and Network Marketing?

Firstly, beware of scams. There are so many crap ads and pages out there that promise the world on a golden platter and ensure you will be rich. That is a load of bull! Get wise on sniffing out the scams; they truly stink a mile away. It can't be said enough, 'if it seems too good to be true, it probably is!'

Then we get into companies that are not scams, but really don't offer any value or depth at all. I'm not slamming any particular brands here, but it's hard to get your heart behind selling absolute junk that doesn't make anyone's life better. Examples being- 'magic' weight loss wraps, overpriced candles, weird pills, nail stickers…you get my point. There are so many quick fixes and false promise gimmicks that make my eyes roll each time I see a post about them. They literally give the entire industry a bad name with their low quality products, cult like recruiting techniques and 'just in it for the sale' mentalities.

That being said, there ARE some super legit Network Marketing companies that are great to run on the side and can result in true income. We know because we spent the last 4 years building my husband's online health and fitness business from $0 to SIX figures. It's not overnight and it doesn't happen without putting major effort into it, but it's literally one of the best ways to build a side income.

Many Network Marketing companies already have the business model set up for you, no need to carry inventory, work on invoicing, or even customer service calls, all of that is provided for you. You just need to align with a company that speaks to your core values.

For us, that was health and fitness, helping others get in amazing shape, and creating a supportive and positive community.

In fact, a recent stat shows that 80% of women in North American that earn over $100,000 a year, are doing it with some form of Network Marketing company.

If the company improves the lives of others, has a real valuable product or service and isn't all about 'selling', then it will likely be a good fit for you.

I have good friends in several different Network Marketing companies that are not only able to support their families, but they are making a positive difference in the world.

I can get behind that any day of the week!

WORKBOOK 17

Everyone should have a secondary stream of income.
Make a goal for yours *(even if you don't know what you will do yet)*. **What would you like to make in the first year, second year and even the fifth year?**

What would hitting those income goals mean for your life, or your family's life? **What could you do that you are unable to do now? What new experiences could you afford?**

Is your secondary dream job *(or primary job)* in the traditional route, working for someone else with location based freedoms, or working totally for self being 100% location independent?

Write down ANY of the jobs mentioned above that you think you might enjoy. Feel free to add any you've thought of on your own.

Printable & Editable Version at traveloffpath.com/workbooks

18 - Building Your Own Empire

If you hate working for the man and want to make your ideas come to life, you can always start your own business from the ground up. It might even be in one of the categories listed above! Sounds scary, but it doesn't have to be. Everyone has their own strengths, interests and skill sets that would inspire a kick ass business to be born. There are no rules when creating your own business, which gives you free reign to get as creative as possible!

What are you MOST passionate about? What makes your heart race? If you had unlimited time and money, what would you be doing with yourself each day?

Starting your own business can be one of the most grueling, yet ultimately rewarding things you will ever do. To minimize the moments that you want to slam your head against the wall, I would highly suggest creating a business that revolves around your passions. If you are doing something you LOVE, you have a lot more patience, focus and energy to stick with it.
BOOM! The birth of a business.

If you can solve a problem using your skills that revolve around your passions, you are destined for great things! Also, if you can make money doing something you are passionate about, you'll never work another day in your life.

My philosophy is that life is too short to do something you hate. I always felt a level of dissatisfaction when I worked in careers where I had no creative contribution. Even when I climbed the corporate ladder and landed my 'dream job' as a Finance Manager for a dealership, it never gave me the sense of achievement I was looking for.

I'm an entrepreneur through and through, even if I've tried to push it down in the past in order to stick within the status quo. My parents always had new businesses, ideas, shops and ventures that had us kids moving around to new cities and schools. In my 20's, I thought I wanted out of the entrepreneurial gypsy life, but as we can both see, I'm right back where I'm meant to be.

But how does my passion turn into cash?

There is no way for me to know what floats your boat or what kinds of skills you have, but here is an idea to get your brain juices flowing. For this example, let's just pretend you love to bake delicious vegan desserts and you would ultimately love to do something as a full time career that revolved around that passion.

- ***Start by doing what you love:*** Bake! Share your finished products, ideas, and daily lifestyle around baking vegan treats with the world and start to build an audience. You could make a YouTube channel with a daily or weekly cooking show, curate an Instagram account with photos and details on your delectable treats, or even start a blog about your vegan lifestyle.
- ***Attract and Engage:*** Next you want to build a following. Ask questions, tell your story, teach people about being vegan, entertain and educate. Start seeking out other vegans and people who live a healthy lifestyle and start engaging on their social media. Get the conversation started.
- ***Monetize:*** After you start building a following and continue to offer them value, you can start to make money. Sell 5-15 second ads on your videos, publish a cookbook, freelancer write for large cooking magazines and blogs, open a vegan bakery, host vegan baking lessons, acquire sponsorships from vegan brands you love by making posts for a fee, etc. The possibilities are endless!

Consistency, patience and determination are the ingredients that turn a passion into a profitable business. Every new venture will take time before you start making money, so the best thing you can do is keep your eye on the prize and spend each day getting one step closer to that goal.

WORKBOOK 18

Step One: 'Know Your Passions'
Back in Chapter 6 you made a list of the things that made you happy. Grab it. Add to it. Even if it doesn't seem 'business' related write it down anyway! Think about things that you are deeply passionate about or things that have always sparked your curiosity in a manner you can't ignore.

Step Two: 'Skills, Education, Experience'
Make a list of the skills, education, training, qualities and experience you have. It could be very technical, like "I have my masters in French literature" right down to "I'm a good listener." Give yourself a break and be honest! This is not a time to hold back and be humble.

Step Three: 'Find a Problem'
It has been said that if you can identify a problem in a particular market, and how to solve it, you will have a super successful business. Looking at both your 'happiness' and 'skill' lists, brainstorm different problems that might exist in the different industries you see.
(Example: Let's pretend your list says you love trees, mountains, sunsets, animals, you have some photography experience, basic web design knowledge and you enjoy teaching people new skills. A problem that might exist around photography and nature: People don't know how to get started with nature and landscape photography. A problem that might exist around website design and learning, in relation to photography: Most photography teachers don't have interactive learning based websites set up. People don't have time or money to attend a traditional photography class.)

Step Four: 'Your Solution'
Come up with solutions to the problems you brainstormed above. Your solutions should come from a combination of your passions, skills and experience. What knowledge, skill or drive do you have to solve the problem you identified? *(Example Solution: You could create a 10 step online nature and landscape photography course that teaches people the skills they need to take better pictures on their own time, for much less than a traditional classroom setting.)*
That example uses your hypothetical skills to solve a problem the end consumer has and creates an opportunity for you.

Part Time Hustle until you're Full Time Ready

Like I mentioned before, creating your own business is by far the most rewarding career choice you could ever make (in my humble opinion). There isn't a day I would trade with my former self who was miserable under the constant eye of the corporate world. Whenever people ask me for advice on whether they should start their own business, I want to shake them and scream at them "Yes, yes YESSSS!!!!!!!" But that googly eyed enthusiasm does come with a caveat.

Don't try and have a full time biz, with full time pay, right out of the gate. No one ever has launched a brand new business or started down a brand new path and the next day was totally profitable and kicking ass. It's a process and a labour of love. It takes time and money and effort to get out of the red and into the black. For this reason, try doing your new business venture part time or on the side of your main gig.

I've seen people dive head first into their idea, only to come up choking for air a few months later. They severed their full time income, abandoned their job, and are trying to make the new business profitable as quickly as possible. This is an enormous amount of pressure for anyone to be under. If you can't pay the bills, you are going to have to give up on the new business and crawl back into the office with your tail between your legs.

My advice is to start building your new business on the side, in your spare time, while you still have your regular employment.

If you do decide to work on your new venture part time, actually work the thing! Flirting with your idea on the weekends isn't going to accomplish diddly squat, you'll have to ferociously attack it every spare chance you get. A part time hustle can make you full time FREE a lot sooner than you think if you truly give it your all.

Funny story: In the spirit of full disclosure, I did NOT follow my own personal advice. I quit real estate cold turkey and had zero clue what I would do next! It sure lit a fire under my ass, but in retrospect, I could have saved myself a few tears.

Remember how I mentioned that NO business is profitable right away? Well, I learned that the hard way. Even though I did start making a small income within a few months, it wasn't enough to support me fully.

I actually cashed in some RRSP's (I know, I know, bad girl!) and used that money to live off of and invest back in my business. Was it risky? You bet! I could have lost all of that money and then I would have been royally screwed. Fortunately for me, I used that pressure as motivation to succeed and it worked! I'm lucky to have been born to parents that instilled a 'failure is not an option' mindset, along with a voracious work ethic. I will never put anything less than everything I've got into my work.

Connecting with other entrepreneurs:

If you know that you want to start your own business, but are totally lost in your own head about it, talk to someone who has 'been there, done that'. Connecting with other people who have already started a successful business is a great way to start learning new ways of thinking. Most entrepreneurs are an ocean of knowledge that can help guide you in the right direction. Plus it's always nice to bounce your idea off someone who will tell you straight up if they think it's bonkers, or if you have a money making idea on your hands.

There are multiple Facebook groups, entrepreneurial hubs, digital nomad forums and business clubs you can be a part of. Some are free and some you pay to be in. Both can be mega helpful!

Another great way to connect with other biz minded people is to follow them. Not like, follow them home in the shadows (you stalker!), but rather follow them on social media!

Success leaves clues and successful people drop lots of them on their blogs, Instagram posts, newsletters, podcasts and videos. Follow and engage with them, ask them questions, and consume their content that is relevant to you. I have learned tons of different things by virtually hanging around with other boss babes.

More of a face to face person? Every city around the world has a co-working space and entrepreneur meet ups. Even chamber of commerce events can be a great way to meet other like minded people in the flesh.

Getting a Mentor

I have always been an 'I'll do it myself' kind of gal. I like learning on my own time and teaching myself new skills. I love brainstorming business ideas and figuring out complex problems that I can solve alone. I'm intensely introverted and I tend to shut out the outside world when left to my own devices. While it's a great thing to be independent, it's not good to think I have the insight to teach myself all the things I will need to be successful.

This is why it's always been imperative for me to get a mentor throughout different stages of my life.

A mentor is someone who can fill in the holes of your ideas, put a little polish on your dusty plans, guide you towards your goals in a way you couldn't see yourself, and give you a little kick in the ass. I've been getting a kick in the ass from someone I admire, 'Boss Babe' CEO, Natalie (Diver) Ellis. Our meetings have become the highlight of my week and have helped me move forward into this next stage of my career. I can only explain what happens inside my brain as a 'fog'. I might be thinking about a certain idea or venture for weeks and this thick, dense fog will roll into my brain. Without her third party opinion, I likely would have made unnecessary mistakes.

Mentors can cost a pretty penny, but in my experience they have been worth every cent. They say it takes money to make money and I know that to be true.

When someone starts a new salaried job, it usually means they have attended school for years of education, which also came with tens (if not hundreds) of thousands of dollars invested.

That person would also likely undergo some sort of new hire training, which again, is time and money invested into learning how to properly do their job.

As a self-employed person, I didn't go to school and spend hundreds of thousands of dollars, nor did I get any 'new hire training', so it's up to me to ensure I am properly investing my time and money into my career.

The investments I have made into mentors have helped me turn ideas into profits and dreams into realities. If we were all born with the knowledge to succeed on our own, then all of us would already be operating billion dollar businesses.

I am never done learning.

A mentor should:
- Keep you accountable
- Be straight up with you
- Help to guide you in the right direction
- Fill in the gaps of your limited knowledge or experience
- Share their point of view
- Aid in clearing 'the fog'
- Be a resource
- Care about your success
- Help you identify your strengths and skills
- Inspire you to take action

Best way to find a mentor:
Reach out to someone who you admire, that also has a proven track record of running a successful business. Most high performers will already have mentorship opportunities set aside for eager people that want help with their ideas.

I personally set aside time for mentoring a maximum of three people each month. I know that taking on more than three people to mentor each month would be putting too much extra work on myself and wouldn't leave me mentally available for them. I also make sure I hire my own mentor for at least one month each quarter. I love the accountability, creative brainstorming and forward leaps that happen when I put my head together with someone I can learn from.

Things I wished I knew before becoming an entrepreneur

It's about helping others FIRST
When people go into a business only thinking about how much money they're going to make, they will usually fail miserably. Successful businesses are the ones who offer a solution to a problem, and set out to improve the lives of others. Greediness leaves a certain stench that catches on after a while.

I once approached an online business with ONLY an income figure in mind, and guess what, it never worked. At first I couldn't understand WHY this amazing idea wasn't taking off like gangbusters, and then I realized it was because I was putting ME first, not the other way around. The moment I changed my mind-set about this and made helping others the first priority, is when I became successful. Help others and the income will happen naturally.

There is no clocking out
If I miss anything about the ol' 9-5 grind, it would have to be the perk of clocking out and getting to leave work behind. As an entrepreneur, there is no clocking out. If a client wants an order at 1:00am and you need the income, guess who is up in the middle of the night working? YOU are!

I am working while I am on vacation, at the airport, in the car, even sitting and watching a movie with Trevor. Yes, there are times when I try and set healthy boundaries for family or 'me' time, but that doesn't happen often.

You will become obsessed
Literally. Every conversation starts to revolve around your business, you scribble things on napkins, take 3978 notes in your phone, even start to strategize in your sleep. Obsessed people get things done and a certain level of obsession is definitely required to stand out in the crowd.

Engagement is key

I could have the best idea, product, website, social media or service in the WORLD, but if I am not out there engaging with my potential clients, they will never like, know or trust me. Engaging and starting a conversation with an audience is a key factor in running a successful business. This includes asking great questions, leaving room for conversations to take place and also seeking out others to engage with. Engagement doesn't happen on its own, it requires you to get out into the world (even digitally) and start talking to people!

Just because you're open for biz, doesn't mean anyone cares

When I made one of my first websites I remember hitting 'publish' to make it live for the world to see…and then hearing crickets.
I didn't understand! I worked so hard on the website, logos, and branding for months, yet there was no one paying any attention! Why didn't they care as much as I did? Because it's not their business! Not everyone will even like your business and that is okay. You don't need 100% of the population to be your potential client. You won't get anywhere trying to cater to everyone. Pick a niche and keep promoting yourself consistently.

People won't 'get it' at first

I still don't think my parents understand what I do, and they are entrepreneurs themselves! Friends, acquaintances and especially family will look at you with all kinds of doubt or confusion. That's cool, it's not their life. You might try explaining your idea until you're blue in the face and they still won't understand. Just leave it be, continue to work on your ideas, and SHOW them what your business is really about with your results.

Spend less time planning, more time doing

Weeks can go by planning for different ways to launch a business, and then guess what, no business ever gets launched. Perfectionism is the killer of all creative ideas.
If I plan long enough, I can talk myself out of anything! (And I have many times before)
I wish I'd known to plan 90% less and instead, just DO 90% more!

It takes time. And money

It will take longer than you think, and it will cost you more than you think, but WOW is it going to be worth it!

There have been so many roadblocks or obstacles I couldn't anticipate that ended up costing me weeks or even months' worth of time. Same thing happened with budgets and investing into the biz, there are always unexpected costs, both small and big, that jump out and take me by surprise. If I had been concentrating on the short game, these things would have totally thrown me off course. By focusing on the long game and the big picture, I KNOW in my heart I will make up the time and the money.

Taking all of the above into consideration, the only thing I wish I had done differently is:
Start Sooner.

Part Six

TRAVEL

19 - Drool Worthy Bucket List

Travel is a huge part of my life. It always has been and always will be. There is something so magical about travel that I can't quite put my finger on. It might be the way it makes me look at things with the wondrous eyes of a child, or maybe in the realization that a major life goal has just been met. It might even be the escape from reality. Whatever it is, I can't get enough of it.
Culture, language, architecture and food, are just some of the things I look forward to each time I find myself in a new destination, but those interests are becoming an ever-growing list!

There are over 190 countries in the world.
Doesn't that just blow your mind? That is over 190 chances to do something you've never done before and see things you've never seen before.
I'm not much for 'counting countries' and keeping numerical tabs as I travel, because what really counts as having 'visited' a particular country? Is it 24 hours within its borders? A week stay? What about a layover?
Instead of counting countries, I would rather keep track of the places that made an impact on me and go from there!
I can't think of anything I would rather be doing other than traveling the world with my husband.

Make Your Bucket List

This is the fun part! Now that your expenses are down, debt is being crushed or has been obliterated completely, you need to know where you are going!
The destinations you put on your bucket list should excite you, scare you, make you curious, and get your heart pumping a little bit.

Are you a city discoverer with a major love for buildings and architecture, a culture hunter who loves language, history and the path less traveled, a beach bum who needs high tides and good vibes, or maybe a mix of everything!

Making a bucket list helps your travel goals to become a reality much sooner, by giving you a visual list of things you want to accomplish. If words motivate you, write your list down inside a journal, on a white board by your desk, or in the notes section of your phone. If you are a visual person, try making a photo collage on the wall, your computers desktop or screen saver, or a virtual Pinterest board. Whatever floats your boat!

A good bucket list should be a mix of different cities and countries you want to see and new experiences you want to have! It's not all about a particular destination, but more about WHY you want to visit that destination or the experiences you imagine yourself having there. "Eating an eclair under the Eiffel Tower" is much more powerful than "Paris".

What do you want to learn, taste, see, touch, feel and hear? Get all of your senses involved while you day dream your list!

Remember there is no minimum or maximum or how many items should be on your bucket list. Same goes for timing. You can aim to do the goals on your list over the next 1, 2, 5, 10, or 20+ years, spread them out so you don't group them all together in the 'One Day' file. A great way to actually start making progress on your list is to figure out which dreams you will tackle FIRST.

If you are already an avid traveler your brain likely already thinks in 'bucket list', but if you are a total newb to global wandering, you might need some inspiration.

Bucket List Inspiration

Bookmark a few of your favourite travel blogs in your internet browser. (Make a folder to find everything easily later on). Seeing real people visit countries, their itineraries, the hotels they stayed in, etc. will give you a great idea of what's possible.

Pinterest. Just like you can use Pinterest to house your own board, it's also a great source of inspiration! There are SO many visually stunning pins out there with ideas for your next vacay. Start an inspiration board and pin your little heart out.

Facebook Groups. There are tons of groups out there for any type of traveler. There are 'female solo travelers', '35+ travelers', 'black travel', 'trailer travel', whatever your interest is, there will be a group to accommodate it! These groups are peer groups where people swap travel ideas, ask questions, and tell their travel stories. Join some based on your interests!

Social Media. Follow some travel bloggers and travel inspo accounts on Facebook & Instagram. On both platforms, you can 'save' a particular post so you can start your own collection of travel stories, destination ideas, and just general drool worthy travel pics.

Old school media. When you read books and watch movies and think "omg that sounds/looks like an amazing place", jot that sucker down on your list.

Start asking friends and family what has been the top places they have visited. People who have 'been there, done that' can give you some great insight on some new places to go. Invite some friends over for drinks and pick their brain on places they've loved.

I used to be afraid to share things on my bucket list with others.
I felt like if I showed it to other people and then I never got around to it, I would feel like a failure. I would just dismiss any cool travel idea that came my way because of worry what others might think. But what was also happening is I wasn't letting myself DREAM enough.

Now I see life is TOO short to design my life around others! *(Ain't nobody got time for that!)*
If I want to experience more things in life, I have to be LOUD about it!

Write it down.
Make a list.

Share it with others!

Here are a few things on my bucket list that I wanted to share with you:

- Ballroom dance at a formal gala in Austria
- Take a transatlantic ocean liner on the same route the Titanic did
- Learn to speak Italian & Romanian *(in Italy and Romania of course)*
- Stay overnight in an ancient Scottish castle
- Take a sleeper car train across Canada
- Volunteer with elephants in Thailand
- Visit Giraffe Manor in Kenya
- Tour the colorful streets of Morocco
- Fly in an Air Emirates suite

(There are hundreds more, but that is just scratching the surface!)

When you make your bucket list, be mindful to share it with others. Not only will it hold you more accountable, but it might inspire the people around you to take action on their own list.
If no one has mentioned this before, you are going to die.
Hopefully your time comes later rather than sooner, but it's inevitable. **Get working on your list now.**

WORKBOOK 19

Your Top 25 Bucket List Goals:

1 Year:

2 Years:

5 Years:

10 Years:

20+ Years:

Now that you have started on your bucket list, I wanted to make sure you are savvy on how to get the best deals possible! Even saving 20% on things like flights and hotels can mean you are traveling more than you ever thought possible.

Get Good at Creeping for Deals

You know how you once spent 2 hours on Facebook creeping your ex and their new squeeze and you got sucked into this time warp of obsession? That is the exact same vortex I get pulled into when I am looking for travel deals. I am consumed. And it's a good thing! I have found incredible flights, hotels, and more for waaaaaayyyyyyy less than they normally go for.
Seriously! There have been times when a hotel was $300 a night across the board on every single website for months and months, yet somehow I grabbed it for $150 a night.
If you really want to have luxury and out of the world experiences without spending the entire contents of your bank account, then creeping is a skill you will want (need) to learn.

Thinking outside the box

Sometimes when I stretch my mind a little bit, cool ways of traveling pop up that I never even thought of! Let me give you an example of one I came across just recently.

So my husband and I will be in the UK this fall and we want to head to Florida or Mexico for Christmas. Looking at premium economy or business class flights, we saw we could get them for around $900 a person. Stay with me here…
Then we watched Titanic (because, well who doesn't love that movie?). Trevor looked at me and said "Hey! I wonder if they still do that! You know, ships that carry passengers across the Atlantic!"
Low and behold, they DO!
An inside cabin room on an Ocean liner from the UK to Florida is about $900 a person, same as flying, but here is the coolest part:

That includes 1 WEEK of fine dining, accommodation, shows, concerts, dance lessons, tennis matches, and more. This ship has a gym, pools, casino, bars, clubs, a library and tons of other things to do and see.
So… obviously this is a WAY better deal! A whole weeks' worth of experiences for the same price as a flight.

Think about how many other types of experiences you can have if you just thought outside the box a little?
Maybe there is a train you can take to a nearby city where the flights are cheaper to depart from. Or perhaps if you take that 24 hour layover in some foreign city the flight is 50% less.

Another great example of this is flying with Qatar Airlines! They allow you to extend your layover in Doha for up to 72 hours without charging you anything extra on your airline tickets. If you only want to stay 24 hours, in some cases they will even pay for your hotel and take you on a complimentary city tour, making it a no brainer! Why wouldn't you take the opportunity to see an amazing place like Doha for free!?

Get that brain dreaming up some out of the box ideas! The world is your oyster!

20 - FLY

Saving on Flights

Flights are a whole different animal.
I'm going to be really honest with you, so don't judge me…. ***I hate economy seats.*** I just do. They are stuffy and crappy and that whole 'omg, if I am stuck in the middle seat for 10 hours I am going to kill myself' kind of terrible. But as of yet I haven't figured out how to print my own money, so economy flights often happen anyway.
But that doesn't mean I don't look for ways out of them… constantly….
I spend 99% of my time looking for premium economy and business class flight deals. Do I always find them? Hardly! It's a cruel, cruel world out there where an economy seat to London might be $200 and a business class seat is $4000 and my extra leg room fantasies are crushed.

If you are like me and getting bumped to first class is akin to winning the lottery, here is what I do to try and score amazing seats on planes (no not snakes on a plane, seats!).

Business Class

I book the economy seats and try to upgrade. Most airlines will let you upgrade at check in, IF they have seats available. If I am booking a plane a few days to a few weeks out, I will do a 'seat preview' to see how many first class seats are sold. If they are 70% unsold, I will book my economy seats on THAT plane in particular (so yes, having flexible dates helps).

Then at check in I make sure I am online EXACTLY 24 hours prior and see if I can upgrade. It usually will only cost $100-$200 extra, which is LITERAL INSANITY considering those seats usually cost $1000-$2000 more than economy if booked in advance.

I use points to upgrade. Many times I have been able to use airline points to either book the biz class ticket up front, or upgrade my economy ticket. You need a LOT of points to do this, so usually it's a year's worth of point hoarding to accomplish this feat, but completely worth it.

I spend hours and hours on Google Flights. If you don't use Google Flights you are missing out! I can put in that I am looking for 'premium economy' or 'business class', a general date range, if its 1 way or roundtrip, etc. Then I scan over weeks and months of different dates to see if there is an anomaly price (and yes this does happen). By doing this, I found a 'lie flat pod' going from Vancouver to Sydney, (roundtrip) that was normally $5000-$6000 **for $750.** Ummmmmm… is this real life!? You get a bed on a freaking plane for the same cost as a middle seat economy ticket. *#winning!*

Another great way to afford business class:
Save, put it into perspective, and just go for it.
I know I'm quite a lone wolf in this, but there are times when I can completely justify spending a ridiculous amount of money on a first class flight. Why? Because I don't spend my money on cable tv, excessive shopping, interest payments on credit card debt, etc. If I told 99% of people that I just spent $8000 on a lie flat pod on Quantas to Austrailia, they would say I have lost my freaking MIND! Honestly, I would probably get hate mail lecturing me on being irresponsible with money and how I should be spending it on other things instead. My answer to that is- Like what? Like paying hundreds of thousands of dollars in interest to a bank? Or spending $20,000 on a daily Starbucks habit over 10 years? No thanks! The average person in North America is spending THOUSANDS a year on just credit card debt interest alone, yet no one is lecturing them.

One of my great passions in life is looking at 787 configurations and the types of suites available on an A380. So while some might splurge for that $4000 Louis Vuitton bag, I'm overjoyed to save up for the flight of a lifetime!

Economy Flights

Okay if you are not high maintenance or an AV nerd and you just want to fly economy and get awesome deals, here are your tips:

Same as above, **make Google Flights your new bestie.** You guys are going to find the most amazing destinations! You can put in your departure airport and leave the 'destination' airport open ended! Then you can set a max budget of, let's just say $300, and it will show you on a MAP where in the world you can fly for $300!!

Be as flexible with dates as you can and you will find flights that are cheaper than you could ever imagine!

Flight alerts. There are many flight alert sites and groups out there that send out an email when a really, really great flight price comes out (like the $157 flight to the UK we just booked). If you can book a trip with last minute notice, even more of these 'alert' type deals will work for you!

Look into price guarantees. Some airlines will guarantee that if the price goes any LOWER than when you first booked, they will refund you the difference. Keep a watchful eye on tickets you've already paid for to see if there are any additional savings to claim.

Airline Loyalty Programs

It's a total waste to book a flight without taking advantage of airline points!
They are free to collect and you can redeem them for things like: free flights, free upgrades and other airline perks.

Unless you fly a ton internationally, you might just want to sign up for your local carriers loyalty programs for now.

You can always create a free account under any of the airlines loyalty programs if you find yourself taking an unexpected international flight.

Canada and US

Air Canada Aeroplan
Alaska Airlines Mileage Plan
American Airlines AAdvantage
Delta SkyMiles
Frontier EarlyReturns
JetBlue TrueBlue
Southwest Rapid Rewards
United Mileage Plus
West Jet Rewards

Aus & NZ

Qantas Frequent Flyer
Air New Zealand Airpoints
Virgin Australia Velocity

International

Air France/ KLM Flying Blue
British Airways Executive Club
Cathay Pacific Asia Miles
Emirate Skywards
Etihad Guest
Lufthansa Miles & More
Qatar Privilege Club
Virgin Atlantic Flying Club

21 - STAY

How to get amazing deals on hotels

I love to stay in hotel rooms. I am that person who feels the most at home when I check into a suite and place my luggage at the end of the bed. It's my 'zen', a weight off my shoulders and my guilty pleasure. But on the subject of frequent traveling, there is one thing I really don't like about hotels- paying too much for them. Over the years I have developed some great strategies for paying the lowest hotel prices possible.

Top 10 Booking Hacks For The Best Hotel Deals!

#1- Time Is Money
The tortoise wins the race in this game. Without patience and time to put into booking your hotel suite, ALLLLLL of the following tips will mean diddly squat. When you invest your time into researching, comparing and booking, that is when you will score the best deal. In my experience the best deals don't usually just pop out of nowhere, I have to hunt them down and be ready to double check my work. Think of what the value is for you if you did save a few hundred bucks on a hotel stay. Is it worth spending an hour or two with 10,000 browser tabs open? For me the answer is YES.

#2- Try Off Season or Shoulder Season
I do this ALL the time! If I really want to stay in a specific hotel or visit a certain city that is usually out of budget, I consider their peak season.... and then avoid it like the plague!
It gives me a headache thinking about paying double and being squashed amongst tons of other tourists in the middle of an area's 'busy season'.

Just because it's the 'off' or 'shoulder' season does not mean it is bad. In some cases the weather might be more tolerable, the attractions easier to see, and just a more relaxed pace of life.

For example, I visited New Orleans in July, dead smack in the middle of their off season. Yes, it was hot, but I like that! Hubby and I got a great deal on our suite at the Windsor Court because we didn't try and book it between February and May, which is their busiest time.

#3- *Compare, Compare, Compare*

Here is where you invest a little bit of time, and if you are anything like me, you will have multiple tabs open and a notebook to jot down price differences.

Hotel Comparison sites are where it's at. This might be the tip that saves you the MOST out of all of them (if you are willing to do the work).

Here is what you do: Open up the hotels website directly, log into your account with them (or create one) and repeat with the following sites in a new tab (the ones I personally use):

- Hotels Combined
- Trivago
- Hotels.com
- Booking
- Otel
- Priceline

One of those top 6 *(and it's usually always different!)* comes out with the best price, so I check all of them before I book. **Always!** There's another site I check all my research against that has surprised me a few times with being drastically lower: Last Minute Travel Club. They ask that you create a membership profile to use their booking engine, but it's totally worth it!

Here is an example: The Grand Fiesta in Puerto Vallarta, Mexico. I've stayed there a few times recently and guess where I booked it through? Last Minute Travel Club for SURE. I just randomly picked May 2 to May 5 for this example, on the hotels direct website, the rate is $258 and on LMT the rate is $158 for exactly the same room, same amenities. That is $100/night ya'll! What would you do with an extra $100/day on a trip??

When I first came across LMT I thought it was just another site claiming it had low prices, but in some cases it REALLY does in a huge way.

Out of the 7 comparison sites, I use LMT, Hotels Combined, and Trivago the most, as they usually come out cheaper 75% of the time. However, I still have found the occasional cheaper deal on Hotels.com, Booking, Agoda, Otel, and Priceline, so don't rule them out.

Just to show you how different they can be, here is an example of all 7 hotel comparison sites with the Grand Fiesta Americana in Puerto Vallarta (May 2-5)

LMTC - $158
Trivago - $178
Hotels Combined - $184
Otel - $228
Priceline - $312
Hotels.com - $316

I'm not sure about you, but I would be TICKED OFF if I paid $316/night when I could have paid $158 a night. That would equal out to $1000 extra for a week stay. **Brutal!**

One final tip for comparison sites: Be ready to pull the trigger. A good deal can literally be gone 1 hour later, so if you see something that is considerably lower, grab it quickly!

#4- Flexible Dates

If you have the ability to shift your time off a few days earlier or a few days later, it might work out in your favour. This one is a little hard to explain, but here I go:

Sometimes the time you are choosing to be at the hotel runs over a holiday, a busy time, or maybe even a conference. Let's say you want to book 5 nights somewhere and it just so happens that on the fourth night the hotel is at full capacity. The rate for that night will sky rocket your average rate for the entire stay! Avoiding it might save you a ton on the overall cost.

Here is an example of how I used this to my advantage: I wanted to stay at one of my favourite boutique hotels in the world, Villa Premiere, for 1 month. (I know right, tough life) but there were 3 days in that 30 day period that JACKED the entire rate.

I adjusted the trip to avoid those 3 days and the rate came down about 30% overall!

So here is how to apply this tip. If you search your hotel of choice from 'x' date to 'y' date and it's not looking good, try shifting those dates ahead or behind a few days, or perhaps even try searching with 1 night less or 1 night more than originally planned. Example: your goal dates are June 1 to June 10. Also try, May 31- June 9, June 2 - June 11, and maybe even June 1 - June 9.

#5 - Upgrade At Front Desk

Are you a risk taker? If you like the thrill of the chase, then asking for a cheap upgrade at the front desk might be your cup of tea. If the hotel has lots of premium rooms available they may let you have one for A LOT lower than you ever would have found it online.

Here are my tips for asking for an upgrade at the front desk:

- Have a bit of a conversation going first! Ask if they have been busy, because if they say it's a slower time for them, you know right away there is an upgrade with your name on it!
- Never say yes to the first price. I checked into the Westin once and asked what the upgrade cost would be to one of their Junior Suites. He replied with the $80 per night listed price and I asked him if that was his best price for the room. Right away he said "Actually, I can do it for $30". Boom! I paid a base rate, plus $30 more per night for a suite that retails for $200 more than my booking.
- If they are FIRM on their upgrade price, see if an upgrade might be available for half of the time. If you are at a resort for 10 days and they can give you a smoking deal on a huge suite for only 5 of those days, wouldn't you still want it?
- The $20 Trick. Okay, have you heard of this before? I first heard about it in Vegas and thank goodness it worked out wonderfully (the first time at least). I handed my ID to the front desk along with a $20 bill and asked if there were any 'complimentary' upgrades. Low and behold, he put me in a better room without changing the rate. Yahoo! On the other hand, I tried this in Mexico and the front desk agent just took it, smiled at me, and literally put us in the worst room at the hotel. The $20 Trick can do wonders or literally backfire in your face.

#6- Are You Loyal?

Loyalty means a lot in this world and it can certainly pay off with your favourite hotel chain.

One of the downsides with booking on third party sites (like hotels.com and the others I mentioned above) is the hotel chain usually will not give you any loyalty points for your stay. If you are always staying at the same chain, these points can add up fast to free meals, complimentary upgrades and even free nights! IF the price of booking the hotel room directly with the hotel chain is at par with the booking comparison sites, book direct to get points! If there is a major price difference, I would personally rather save money than accumulate points.

Here are my best loyalty tips for booking directly with hotels and why in some cases it's the best idea:

- Sign IN! When you sign in to the hotel loyalty program directly, you may be able to see 'members only prices' which can be deeply discounted.
- If you love a brand/chain, stick with them! Points can add up fast if you are not collecting them from every different hotel chain under the sun.
- Most big chains have something called 'price matching'. Let's use Marriott for example. They claim they will beat any price by 25%. Which is HUGE! The only downside is they require you to submit the claim showing the site you found the cheaper deal on has exactly the same cancellation policy and they take 24 hours to get back to you. On many of the hotel comparison sites, 24 hours is enough time to see that cheap price disappear forever. You also must BOOK the hotel room with Marriott when you submit, so if they can't 'find' that sweet deal you saw, you now have a full price Marriott room with your name on it.
- Loyalty can also mean turning airline points into hotel chain points, which many frequent fliers do. Make sure you have the best credit card and points accounts for all the major airlines and hotel chains to swap points around as you need to.

#7- Know What You're Getting Into

Don't use Hotwire, Priceline Auctions, and other sites that don't tell you the name of the hotel until you have booked it with no way out.
I know this goes against everything else you read when you google how to get hotel deals. Most people say "Oh try that site where you grab a last minute deal and the hotel name is secret, but you can get 5 star hotels for half price."
No. I am calling total BULL on this method.

You know what, in some cases it may have worked out for people, but in my experience I pay less using my 7 key comparison sites or asking for an upgrade at the hotel.
I tried the 'secret hotel' way and it's not fun. They tell you it's a 4 Star and it's really the 3 Star down the road from the 4 Star that you actually wanted to stay at. The devil you know is better than the one you don't. If you only have a few weeks of vacation a year, why gamble that you might spend it in a place you really don't enjoy that you also likely paid normal rates for.
Puerto Vallarta is a city I know like the back of my hand and I played the 'Hotwire' game there a few times and regretted it. Now I can actually look at the hotels on that site and know which one they are referencing and I can find the same deal on LMTC or Hotels Combined.
Sorry if Hotwire is your jam, but it's certainly not mine!

#8- Collaborations

Say what??? Okay this tip might only be applicable to a smaller group of people, but it's a dang powerful one.
There is nothing wrong at all with talking to your dream hotel about a possible collaboration. What I mean by that is - how you may be able to work with the hotel on a great rate, upgrade, or other perk.
Here are some examples:
- If you have a large social media following that includes the people from the hotels target market, they may welcome you to stay for a discounted rate for some social plugs. Like live 'stories' on Instagram, Facebook posts, YouTube video tours, blogs, and other viral promotional methods. Billboards, commercials and magazine ads are expensive! Hotels know a discounted rate or a free upgrade has way more value if you have an audience that will enjoy it.

- Reviews. A newer hotel or a smaller independent hotel might not have any reviews up yet. Reviews are the life blood of the industry, so perhaps ask them what they would be willing to do if you provide a detailed review with pictures and video. Again, if it's a small hotel, maybe they even need photos of the rooms done and you happen to be a photographer. Works out perfectly!
- For these tips, of COURSE your opinion of the hotel cannot be swayed by their generosity. You have to be upfront with them that your opinion is your own and the benefits they might offer you will not change your point of view. Honesty is the best policy.

#9- Coupon Codes & Email Signups

Sometimes there is STILL money on the table even after you have found an incredibly low price!

Email Sign-Ups: Remember how in tip #3 I told you about hotel comparison sites? Well it just so happens that Otel has an extra perk when you sign up for their email list. I found a killer deal on a hotel in New Orleans on Otel and then filled out their 'subscribe for 6% off' email sign up form at the bottom of the page. Within about 10 minutes I was emailed a coupon code that gave me an additional 6% off that booking that was already lower than any other site. Winning!

Coupon Codes: When in doubt, GOOGLE IT! Just type in 'so and so hotel coupon code'. Sometimes you can find one and other times it just leads you around in circles of junk (I think it's worth it in the end).

Price Alert Sites: There are a few out there that email you if your hotel rate goes down, when major brands have promotions on, etc. I find these can get overwhelming if I am not traveling for a while, but super helpful when I'm in 'booking mode'.

#10- Diamond in the Rough

We all want super big suites for lower prices, am I right? Well sometimes the WORST place to look for a hotel deal is at the fancy 4 and 5 star chains. Stay with me on this one....

If you are looking for a suite that is big, unique, and fabulous, you can sometimes find a diamond in the rough at the most unexpected property.

For this example, I am going to show you a suite we recently found in Kelowna, BC, Canada. The hotel was not 'rough' by any means, but it certainly is not in the upper echelon of local upscale resorts. It's called the Comfort Suites, part of the Choice Hotels brand and is your typical highway hotel. BUT, it has an incredible, massive, luxurious, and insanely unique honeymoon suite that is only about $30 more than the basic room (and about $400/n LESS per night than other suites in fancy dancy nearby resorts that were comparable in size). I was blown away by how grand the suite was and how low of a price it came in at. That's what they call VALUE folks!

Moral of the story: try downgrading the star of property and upgrading the type of room for a deal that is sure to impress.

Hotel Loyalty Programs

Loyalty programs are the cat's meow!
They are free to set up, allow you to earn points on your stays and usually give additional benefits like: free Wi-Fi, breakfast, late check out and every 4th night free.

I am a member of every single loyalty program below. I organize all the membership numbers and passwords inside an app on my phone called 'StoCard'. I opt out of the promotional emails (otherwise I would be getting dozens a week) but before a trip I always check what deals or promotions they have going on.

When you are super loyal to a brand, the points add up faster than you would think! Trevor and I use points for free hotel stays at least 3 times a year!

Here are some of the hotel loyalty programs I'm a part of:

Starwood SPG
IHG Rewards
Marriott Rewards
Hilton Hhonors
Wyndam Rewards

Best Western Rewards
Club Carlson
Choice Privileges
Fairmont President's Club
World of Hyatt
La Quinta Returns
Leaders Club
Omni Select Guest
Stash Hotel Rewards
Le Club AccorHotels
Kimpton Karma Rewards
iPrefer Hotel Rewards
Discovery
Fiestamericana
Small Luxury Hotels
Sandos 4 U
Jumeriah Sirius
Trump Card Privileges
Hotels .Com Rewards
Orbitz Rewards
Last Minute Travel Club Rewards

Vacation Rentals

Hotels are great for having a full service experience, but they can get pretty pricey for extended stays! We have found that for trips 7 days or more, vacation rental sites will get you more square footage for less than a hotel.

Most vacation rentals have a 3 or 4 night minimum, so they are not ideal for renting only 1 night, but of course there are exceptions to that rule.

One thing to remember with vacation rental sites is, ALWAYS negotiate. These homes are largely owned by individuals and they want to have their property booked as much as possible.

Pro Tip: Look at the booking calendar. If it's chalked full of rentals, just know you will have less bartering power. If there are some big gaps and empty spots, that is your invitation to get negotiating! Trevor and I have found we can also get a deal if we rent a 2 or 3 bedroom place when we mention it's just the TWO of us. Rental homes get a lot of wear and tear from hosting large groups, not to mention massive utility bills when fully occupied, so they like knowing it's a more relaxed tenant.

Here is a list of my favourite companies to book vacation rentals on:

Homeaway
They also own VRBO, so you are better off using the mother site, homeaway.com to search under both brands at once. For North American users, this has really been the largest and oldest rental site. Even though I use this site to book rentals, I am still blown away by how HIGH I feel prices have climbed. My eyes are regularly popping out of their sockets while browsing.

AirBNB
This rental site has gained a ton of popularity in the last few years! When it first came on the scene, I could notice a big price difference between the listings on its platform compared to Homeaway. Now I am not so sure the same gap exists.
The nice thing about AirBNB is the ability to search for a private room in a larger home, opposed to the entire house itself, which is more popular on Homeaway.
I do find that the same listings will be on both sites, but AirBNB still has some exclusive, more trendy and catering to millennials, type of rentals.

TripAdvisor Rentals *(Also own HouseTrip & FlipKey)*
I use TripAdvisor constantly to ensure the hotel I want to book isn't a total roach motel, so why not the same for their newer addition of vacation rentals! They use the same review and rating system for the rentals as the hotel listings, so it's a nice familiar way to compare homes for rent.

22- Travel Like a PRO

If you love bite sized tips that pack a big punch, this is the list for you! I searched my entire brain, including all my memories and past trips, and compiled the best of the best for you *(it was like the Labyrinth in there guys!)*. If you're reading a paper copy of this book, highlight the ones you love for later!

Kashlee's BEST-EST Travel Tips:

Get an airport lounge pass. When you travel a lot the super-fast Wi-Fi, free snacks, drinks, oversized chairs, quiet cozy corners and even sometimes beds or showers can really make a difference. If I am not in a lounge I am always spending money charging my phone, grabbing a bottle of water, a sandwich, etc and it adds up to more than a lounge pass would anyway. I personally use Priority Pass and I love it!

Pack a scarf or a sarong. You will always find a use for one. You can cover up your bikini when you want to go dining, cover your head at religious attractions, use it as a towel, a sling for an injured arm, shelter from the sun, to save your hairdo from the wind, to wrap up or carry several items, to keep warm, disguise…. The possibilities are endless.

Use the cloud. Lost phones and damaged cameras happen all the time on the road. Whenever you are connected to Wi-Fi, get your precious photos into the cloud so you have duplicate copies. You can also back up videos and large files into a small external hard drive, but if your whole bag gets lost you're SOL. I recently had my GoPro stolen right out of my hotel room in London, and I had JUST turned off the cloud function the day before. If I had kept it on, I would still have all my photos, alas they are GONE. Big lesson learned.

Ear Plugs. I had some made for my ears by an Otolaryngologists *(that's a mouthful!)* and they are super comfortable and practically sound proof. They are great for crying babies on flights, or noisy hotels. Oh, and for Trevor's nonstop snoring.

Eat where the locals eat. It's cheaper, it's home cooked and it's a better representation of the local cuisine. Plus, it's the best place to meet new local friends.

Keep a journal. Time goes by SO fast and there are only so many things we snap pictures of, which are usually only the best parts. Keep a journal of how you feel, both sides of the story, your itineraries, your discoveries, highs and lows, thoughts and lessons learned, and things you saw. There is something about the written word that can take you right back to that moment better than a picture can.

Pack less. Even though I have become pro at this, I STILL find things in my bag I don't use, even on month long trips. Pack, take it down by 50% and then try and cut it down again. A great way to help you decide what you really need is to plan your outfits ahead of time and try and bring pieces that match most of your other clothes.

Don't fill your body with crap 24/7. Just because you are on a trip doesn't mean all your healthy food habits need to fall out of the window. Stop crushing street vendor donuts, sugary sodas and 14 airport lounge cocktails each time you have a travel day. They start to add up and will make you bloated, break out, lose sleep, and just miserable in general. Hunt for healthy snacks and don't give into temptation every time you encounter it, because that will be every few minutes. I keep a healthy bar in my bag to help with this.

Have proof of your onward travels. Some countries require that you show them proof you are leaving at some point. If you booked a round trip ticket, you are already covered. But if you are like ME and love traveling with one way flights, make sure you have proof of your next car rental, train, bus, flight, or boat out of that country. *I got stuck at the Guayaquil airport traveling to Mexico because of this!*

Check Visa requirements. I consider myself very lucky to have been born in a country that gives its citizens such a powerful passport to travel with. As a Canadian citizen I can travel visa free or 'visa on arrival' to 171 countries in total. Travelers from the USA are even more fortunate with 174 countries on their list. Each country has their own visa requirements by destination that everyone should double check before booking travel.

As of Jan 1 2017, Canadians require Visas to enter: Afghanistan, Algeria, Angola, Benin, Bhutan, Brazil, Burundi, Cameroon, Chad, China, Congo, Equatorial Guinea, Eritrea, Ghana, Guinea, Iran, Iraq, North Korea, Liberia, Libya, Mali, Nauru, Niger, Nigeria, Pakistan, Russia, Saudi Arabia, Sierra Leone, Somalia, South Sudan, Sudan, Syria, Turkmenistan, Uzbekistan, Vietnam, and Yemen.

USA is virtually the same and only has these differences: no Visa required for: Equatorial Guinea & Vietnam and Visa required for Venezuela & Cuba.

Look up the good and the bad reviews. I love using Trip Advisor to look up both sides of the story! It's great to try and convince yourself that super cheap hotel will be amazing because you really want to go, but you need to know what you're dealing with! I read a handful of the 5 star reviews as well as the 1 and 2 star reviews. Sometimes there is a pattern (ex- all of the bad reviews were in a certain year and management has now changed) which can sway my decision to try out the hotel after all.

Adaptors. Have a power voltage adaptor for the country you are going to before you actually go. They are so expensive at airports and hotels and you are better off being prepared! Even if your plug fits into International sockets, don't do it! You can fry your device, or worse, start a fire!

Read a book or watch a movie that takes place in your next destination. For example, we visited the UK so we started watching the Netflix series 'The Crown' which gave us so much insight to the history of the monarchy. By watching movies or reading books that are set in the country you are traveling to, you will pick up on local customs, slang, fashion, quirks and other details that the guide books don't teach you.

Ask the locals. Locals have that special degree of insight to answer your specific questions that a fellow tourist wouldn't have.

Keep an open mind. Experiencing new cultures and customs can sometimes feel a little strange, but keeping an open mind and staying curious are the keys to making lasting memories. Not everything has to be exactly like it is back at home. Just go with the flow and be flexible, you never know what you might like until you try it!

After dark rule. Trevor and I have an after dark rule when we travel to a new place, meaning, we don't go out after dark until we have our bearings in the area and until we have established that it is safe. We ask locals, consult guide books, and people watch to see what the other tourists do once the sun goes down. Some places (like in coastal Ecuador) we could go walking after dark in our town with no problem, but traveling by bus at night was a BIG no-no.

Give Back. A lot of travel is take, take, take. When you are visiting a place that has given you nothing but great service, wonderful memories and incredible experiences, ask yourself what you can do to give back. It could be as small as bringing care packages for locals or leaving some of your clothing or books behind. On a larger scale you could volunteer, donate to a foundation, raise funds for a community project or bring awareness to a cause that needs extra help.

Smile. A smile is a universal language. Every country and culture recognizes its warmth and friendly nature. You will be surprised what happens when you simply smile at others during your travels. Plus it cures resting bitch face (which I suffer from).

Wipes. I carry a small pack of anti-bacterial wipes in my purse at all times. They are great for cleaning questionable surfaces all over the globe. I routinely wipe down my seat and tray table on airplanes, dirty tables that I am about to eat on, and anything else I encounter that needs a little disinfecting.

Trust your gut. If something feels wrong, it probably is. If you have a bad feeling about a person, a place or a particular situation, listen to that inner voice. We all have survival instincts that kick in when they sense something that could represent danger and it's not worth putting those signals on silent.

Don't dress like a slob on your flight. That doesn't mean you should we wearing high heels or a 3 piece suit, but those baggy sweatpants and sloppy t-shirt aren't great options either. First off, you will never get a free upgrade to business class if you look homeless, ever. Secondly, what if you have an unforeseen extended layover in a city without your baggage? Do you really want to take an impromptu tour of Rome in your rag-a-muffin robes? Probably not.
Wear comfortable clothing that would also be appropriate if you had a change of plans. Consider what would happen if you lost your luggage and had to wear this outfit for the next 48 hours. Could you go for lunch in it? Meet up with friends in it? Enter establishments in it? If the answer is no, change your outfit.

Tri-lingual menus. If the menu is in 3 or more languages and there are waiters outside trying to lure pedestrians inside, the food probably sucks. Check with a local, look at the highest rated places on TripAdvisor, ask inside a travel group, or just look with your eyes at what restaurants seem to be hopping all on their own.

Make multiple stashes of cash. Bags get lost, wallets get stolen, people get separated. For this reason, never ever, EVER keep all your cash in one place. Make different stashes of local currency in your carry-on, checked bag, on your person, back at the hotel safe, etc. This way if your bag is snatched or you drunkenly make it rain all over a Las Vegas pool party, you have a backup reserve.

Make 2 colour copies of your passport. Leave one at home with a family member or friend and keep one with you in a different bag than your passport.
True story: I was robbed at gunpoint in Nicaragua and they stole my bags, including my passport. Before the trip I left a colour copy of my passport with my brother Cody, telling him it was for 'just in case'.

He teased me to NO end about it, until I actually called him from the Canadian consulate a few weeks later needing him to email it over to them. I had no proof of who I was and I was so thankful I had left a copy with him to expedite the process of getting an emergency passport issued.

Leave an itinerary. If you are traveling for an extended amount of time, or through places where you will not have internet access, leave a copy of your itinerary with someone who isn't on the trip with you. Anything can happen. If there was a natural disaster, a coup, or if you drop off the map for longer than expected, you can still be tracked down and found based on your travel plans.

Don't use outside ATMS. If you find an ATM on the street that is open 24/7 with no security, don't use it. Scammers can easily install card readers to these machines that can steal your information or expose your pin number. Try and use only inside ATM's in reputable banks, hotels, and shopping centres.

Pack a smart carry-on bag. I always pack my carry-on under the assumption that my checked bag WILL be delayed 100%. That ensures I always put a next day outfit, medications, contacts, important papers and anything else I will need for at least 24 hours. Also, if I am bringing something that I would literally break down and cry over if it got lost, it also goes in my carry-on.

Don't do secure things on insecure Wi-Fi. There are few things in life that feel better than finding open, fast and free Wi-Fi when I'm on the road! However, some of those connections are super sketchy, so I don't do shopping, banking, or any other secure action on them. If the Wi-Fi does not require a password, don't do anything on it that could compromise your personal info.

Let your bank know your plans. This one is a dying tip because banks are getting super savvy with their customer behaviour algorithms and start to learn your travel patterns. Trevor's bank on the other hand seems to still be using clay tablets because his cards get flagged nonstop when we travel.

When they see a charge in New Orleans one day and Houston the next, they figure someone has made off with his card and they freeze his ability to make transactions. This doesn't fly when you've just filled up with gas and the cashier tells you your card has been declined. So that you don't end up in super frustrating situations, let your card company know when and where you will be traveling. This way they will know it's you spending $22 on an airport salad in Dubai and not some other idiot.

Get an RFID bag or wallet. Does your credit or debit card have that little chip with the 'tap' feature? Pretty convenient, right? Turns out, it's super convenient for scam artists too. They simply get within a few inches of you with a hidden RFID reader, and you just had your card compromised. This usually happens in crowded places like airports, shopping malls, conference rooms and sporting events. If your bag or wallet has a built in RFID blocker, these arseholes can't get one bit of your information.

TP. Carry toilet paper in your purse or your girlfriends' purse if you are male. You would be surprised at how many places in the world do not have toilet paper in the washroom stalls. Or proper washrooms in general. EEK!

Bring flight attendants goodies. Find out how many flight attendants will be on your next flight and bring an equal number of small presents for them. They are always appreciative of this gesture and it might have you better looked after on the flight as a bonus. Great things to bring are: small puzzle books, lip chap, hand cream, hand sanitizer, pens, mints, chocolates, candy, etc.

Learn some basic phrases. This doesn't mean you have to go all Rosetta Stone and learn how to have an intellectual conversation in 20 different languages. Aim to learn a few basics phrases in the language you will be exposed to, like: hello, thank you, yes, sorry, you're welcome, excuse me, stop, help, how much, I don't speak…etc. Practice them on cue cards before you go and keep a copy on your phone or in your bag. Don't rely on app translators that use Wi-Fi, because when you don't have any data you will be left drawing out pictures and trying to use hand signals.

Get more iron free clothing. Pack pieces that don't need special care or ironing in order to wear. I can't even put a value on an item that can be crammed at the bottom of a bag for days and still looks great when I throw it on.

Have change. Always carry some small coins and change in the local currency. You will need these to buy toilet paper that you forgot to put in your purse, pay washrooms, bus fare, a bottle of water, etc. Many foreign countries will flat out refuse to change your massive bills for tiny items, so don't try and pay for a $1 item with a $20 bill.

Visit the local tourism office. Every city has a tourism office that is full of brochures, coupons, and information about all the events and attractions in the area. Don't feel like you are being a nuisance, it's the actual JOB of the people inside these offices to help you make the most of your trip. Ask them questions, get directions, and learn more about what to see and do.

Take the bus tour. I know they seem really tacky, but those double decker bus tours with the guy on the mic are a really great way to get your bearings in a city! I try and do them on my very first day and it gives me a bird's eye view of the city, lets me learn the core streets and teaches me history about the buildings. The guide will usually point out his favourite attractions, which can be helpful when deciding on what to see next. Also, many bus tours are 'hop on, hop off' which makes it double as transportation throughout the city that day.

Buy groceries and carry snacks. Even if I am at an all-inclusive resort I will find a way to stash some snacks in my room, but I will do a grocery shop for a hotel or rental stay. Being hangry sucks! Eating out every meal is insanely expensive and usually quite unhealthy, so I like to be able to access some good food when I can. If my hotel room has a mini fridge I will grab fruit, yogurt, juice, veggies, etc. I also carry Kind bars, quest bars, unsalted nuts and other snacks on me when I am out and about.

Check out the hostel bars. Don't hate on me for this, but I am not a hostel lover. For an introvert like me, it's not my cup of tea. I value my own space more than getting a killer deal on a room.

However, hostel bars and restaurants can be one of the best places to grab a meal or a drink. Many hostels allow non-guests to use the bars and they are hands down the cheapest places to have a social snack. You can meet people and get some awesome deals on drinks and food, and then retreat back to your private hotel.

Take local transportation. Its way cheaper than a cab and in almost every country it's absolutely safe. Locals take this form of transportation every single day as part of their work and family life, so you know the routes are good and efficient.
I still take cabs sometimes, but I love hoping on a local bus for a few cents and really diving into living like a local.

Have travel insurance. Don't leave the country without it. Ever! It's not worth it. If that trip turned into an $850,000 medical bill, how would that affect the rest of your life? If you don't have the $80 to insure your trip, don't go. Period.
My credit card (TD Infinite Privilege) gives me 22 days of coverage each time I leave the country. I either call them to top it up for longer trips, or I get insurance while I'm actually abroad with World Nomads.

Take a photo of your packed bag. You should have travel insurance and that insurance should cover any items that might get lost or stolen from you. Take a photo of your bag so you have a record of the clothing, electronics and personal items you packed. This will help prove your case if you need to make an insurance claim and will also help you remember the entire list of items you might be missing.

Use your trip delay interruption and cancellation insurance. Most credit cards and travel insurance companies have some nifty features that you should take advantage of! For example, my credit card will pay up to $1000 for expenses if my flight is delayed for more than 4 hours. Say WHAT!? All of a sudden the anger and frustration of a delayed flight turns into "let's go have a meal and check into that hotel, FO FREEEEE". Look into your coverage for having to cancel a flight, lost baggage and other circumstances. You might have more coverage than you thought!

Vaccinations. If you are going to a country that requires a vaccination, plan it out in advance. You might need several rounds of shots over months of time, so don't leave it until the last minute.

Bring a jacket. Even if you are headed to the hottest desert on earth, bring one jacket. You might need to use it for shade, to block wind, or to warm up on an unseasonably cold night. *If I ever travel to the USA in the summer, I bring a thick one…you guys really CRANK the AC!*

Use Seat Guru. If you are cool with being crammed in the worst economy seats and don't give a darn about things like chairs that don't recline, disregard this tip. I am a bit of an AV geek and I love to learn about the configuration of the plane I will be flying on. I use seat guru to spot the best places to sit on the plane BEFORE I buy my ticket. There is usually great advice for crappy seats you can't see from the airlines booking site.

Bring a pen. There is nothing more annoying to a flight attendant than hearing "Can I borrow your pen?" when they are handing out the customs cards. No, you cannot borrow their pen because there are 250 other people on this plane that will want to as well. Have a pen in your carry-on bag. Keep that pen in your everyday bag when you are traveling as well. You will always have a need for it.

Use TEP. Tep Wireless is a little device that gives me fast Wi-Fi all over the world. I can hook up 5 devices to it at once and use social media, video calling, web browsing, emails, whatever. A day pass of unlimited internet is $8, which is way better than trying to use my phones data and getting massive overage or roaming charges. I am also terrified of insecure Wi-Fi and people stealing my info, so I like knowing I am always hooked into a secure network. You can rent a device for your trip, or if you are a frequent traveler like me, you can buy one as well.

Remove all packaging from everything before you pack it in your luggage. I know this sounds a little anal, but trust me, it all adds up! The packaging around your disposable razors, new mascara wand, and especially things like small electronics, have got to go. You would be surprised that they might be adding 1 or 2 pounds to your total luggage, which could have been used for shoes.

Kashlee's Travel Must Haves

Through a lot of trial and error, I have discovered there are certain things I cannot travel without, nor should I have to. I've been stuck in some pretty strange places unable to get basic necessities (like Wi-Fi) and it's literally driven me up the wall. Things like makeup, certain foods, even clothes are easy enough to get in most countries worldwide, but these following items are things I won't go abroad without.

I have contacted some of these brands to secure deals for my readers to try, so take advantage of the discounts! Full disclosure, if you decide to use any of these products or services, I may get a small referral from the brand. That has not, and will never, sway my opinion on what is a good service or product. All opinions are authentic and my own.

DUFL

You have your photos and music in the cloud right? Most people use some sort of cloud service like Dropbox, Evernote, iCloud or Google photos. DUFL is exactly like those virtual cloud services, only with my wardrobe.

I packed up 90% of my clothes and shipped them to my DUFL virtual closet (which really exists in Arizona). They took pictures of each item and put them in an app for me. Each time I want to travel somewhere new, the weather changes, or I just need new outfits, I simply select the items I want and they send it to me. When I am done, I have them pick it up and re-store into my virtual closet. DUFL has my shoes, accessories, clothes, jackets, boots, even a toiletry kit with extra makeup and products I love.

At the time of writing this book, I am having DUFL send my riding boots, trench coats, sweaters and jeans to the UK for me, and I will meet my clothes there upon arriving at my hotel. This way, I don't have to carry MASSIVE bags through the airport, pay for checked luggage, or try and anticipate what clothes I will need. I can always have DUFL send me more or pick up extras in short notice!

They also clean my clothes, so I never have to worry about dry cleaning or laundry as I travel.

They started out as a service for business travelers who could have freshly cleaned suits sent to their hotels and conferences, minimizing waiting for luggage at the airport and making business travel a breeze. Then they started doing the same service for sports enthusiasts, sending golf clubs and surf boards so travelers weren't dragging them through oversized luggage areas. Now, they have seen a rise in nomads like me, who don't want to FLY all the way home just to get different clothes, or try and over pack each time like a crazy person.

There is no limit of how much DUFL will hold for me, and it's only $9.99 a month to store clothing in their facility (which is 1/15th the cost of a storage unit I used to pay for to hold my extra clothes!). During a road trip this summer, I had them send gowns to New Orleans so they didn't get all mangled in the car. I also had them send cool weather clothing to meet me in Newport, Oregon when we went from extreme heat in Arizona to the cooler pacific coast.
The cost to send the clothes to and from locations varies if it's domestic or international, but it's ALWAYS cheaper than dry cleaning them myself, having to buy new items, or of course having to fly home to get them.

When I arrive at my hotel or vacation rental, a piece of luggage with all the requested items is waiting for me! All the clothing is folded neatly with tissue paper to stop wrinkles and they even have a free surprise each shipment! It could be a T-shirt, a premium hair care product, even a healthy organic snack.

I'm obsessed with DUFL and they have allowed me to keep most of my favourite clothes without having to drag them around with me to every country. I cannot say enough good things about them!

DUFL.com
Use code 'Kashlee50' for 50% off your first trip

TEP Wireless

If there is one thing in this world that can make me SNAP, it's not having Wi-Fi. I am an entrepreneur. I need Wi-Fi like I need oxygen.

My business, wellbeing and future depend on my being able to work while traveling. I have literally lost my shit being stuck in places with no Internet, like Ecuador for example. We had rented an ocean front villa for six months that did have decent internet, but the power would go out constantly, sometimes for DAYS. That means no fridge, no hot water for showers, no INTERNET. Imagine what kind of a mood your boss would be in if the entire office lost internet with important deadlines looming. A crazy person, right? That was me.

Because of that experience, I started demanding we have a cell phone for each country that we stayed in, so we could hotspot off it if necessary. A great idea, but get 2 people who use a lot of data hot spotting on 1 cell phone, and you have a nasty bill on your hands.

Enter: TEP!
I found them online and read about 1000 reviews before committing, but I am so glad I did! I got my 4G TEP unit right before a month long road trip in the USA and it worked everywhere I needed it to. The data is $8 a day, unlimited use, and I can hook up to 5 devices at once. That means, my cell, Trevor's cell, my laptop, Trevor's laptop, my iPad. Not having to hang around gas stations trying to hook up to insecure Wi-Fi like crack fiends was a game changer for us.

My sister in law Stacy recently got one to take to Sweden for 2 weeks and was raving about how good it was! She used it on trains, waiting in lines, to look up directions and maps, even to make reservations for dinner. Her and hubby always had a connection to update us all on Instagram and the bill was super small and reasonable compared to what roaming would have been.

You can buy the unit to keep, or simply rent one for a short trip.
Tepwireless.com
Use code 'THMM' for 10% off

Priority Pass

This is a membership program that includes access to over 1000 swanky airport lounges in more than 500 cities worldwide.
Who needs access to lounges? YOU DO.

Sure, there are some mediocre lounges out there that offer nothing but a few free crackers and a quiet spot to sit down away from the chaos, but they are the minority. Most lounges have oversized reclining chairs, charging stations, magazines, hot and cold food, snacks, premium Wi-Fi, even booze for FREE. Some of these joints even have sleeping pods and clean showers available to pass holders. A new benefit just added in 2017 is food and bar credits to restaurants outside the lounge in the main terminals.

These lounges are a little piece of heaven before a flight or during a layover. I am constantly looking forward to relaxing and feeling pampered in my own little oasis. Nothing says "omg pass me a Xanax" like standing in an overcrowded boarding area for hours with kids screaming and people bumping you with their luggage as they walk by. The lounges are my escape.

I actually go EARLY to the airport just to make sure I have enough time to chill for a bit and soak in the VIP experience!

Since the lounges cover things like Wi-Fi, wine, and food, I actually SAVE money with my annual membership, as I am going to buy those things anyway.

Priority Pass has lounges in over 500 cities, but here are a few you might recognize:

Canada- Edmonton, Montreal, Quebec, Toronto, Vancouver, Winnipeg, Calgary

USA- Anchorage, Atlanta, Baltimore, Boston, Chicago, Cincinnati, Colorado, Dallas, Honolulu, Houston, Las Vegas, Los Angeles, Miami, Minneapolis, New York, Orlando, Phoenix, Portland, San Fransisco, San Jose, Seattle, Washington.

_UK-_ Aberdeen, Belfast, Birmingham, Bristol, Cardiff, Derry, Doncaster, Durham, East Midlands, Edinburgh, Exeter, Glasgow, Humberside, Inverness, Isle of Man, Leeds, Liverpool, London, Manchester, Newcastle, Newquay, Norwich, Southampton

AUS/NZ - Auckland, Brisbane, Cairns, Christchurch, Queenstown

Membership rates vary from $99-$399 a year.
PriorityPass.com

Travelon Makeup Bag

I like being organized and this bag sure does that for me! In total high maintenance style, I would commonly tote around way more health and beauty items than one female would ever need. I felt like four different primers and ten different shades of taupe eye shadows was completely necessary. I never have used all the makeup I've brought with me traveling, not even close. Getting this bag actually STOPPED me from bringing so much stuff, as it smartly only has room for actual necessities. I'm impressed with how much I can actually cram into it, but even more impressed with how it taught me to start identifying what I really needed. On my blog I did a 'pack with me' video showing all the makeup, hair products and skin care this bag holds and how it's the greatest makeup bag I've ever owned.

TravelonBags.com
'Kashlee' for 15% off

Arden Cove Anti Theft RFID Purse

The most annoying thing on Earth is to have your credit cards compromised while traveling. If you only have one card, you are essentially screwed until your bank can priority mail you a new one. This is a situation I never want to be stuck in again. A few years ago, my cards got compromised four freaking times and to say it was inconvenient would be an understatement. Never wanting this to happen again, I started digging around for what technology could help protect me from credit card theft. RFID wallets and purses block thieves from using the 'tap' feature on your card to steal info as they walk by you. Great right!? Only thing was, most of the ones I found online were dog ugly. (Think socks and sandals kind of vibe) That was until I ran into Arden Cove, a company out of San Francisco who makes gorgeous RFID bags. Founded and designed by two trendy sisters who are passionate about the safety of traveling women, this was exactly the kind of solution I was looking for.

Not only do they have RFID blocking technology, they are also slash proof, water-proof, have locking zippers and other anti theft features that I love. If you look through any recent pictures of me walking through any city, there is a huge chance I have my Arden Cove bag over my shoulder.
They just launched some gorgeous new styles and you will be stunned at how affordable they are! Gone are the days of overpriced handbags that do diddly-squat for your safety!

ArdenCove.com
'KashleeK' for 10% off!

Ice Roller

One of the best, and insanely affordable, beauty tricks I've ever been taught. My guilty pleasure is following Lauryn Evarts, the creator of popular blog The Skinny Confidential, who is the best source for beauty hacking out there. She turned me onto rolling this small device over my face each morning, straight out of the freezer. So what does it do? It basically does everything. Supermodels get 'ice facials' all the time and swear by it, this is essentially a cheaper version of that, and at $13 I'm all for it!
Beauty Wise: takes out redness, stops puffiness (especially under eyes), makes pores smaller, evens tones, refreshes you, helps circulation, lymphatic drainage, etc.
Health Wise: It helps to soothe pain and muscles and tension. And it's relaxing, so that helps too! The space in my luggage is super limited, but I always have room for my ice roller!

Technology I bring with me around the world full time:

- GoPro Hero Black 5 (side note! Mine was just stolen from my hotel room in London…UGH… so I will be replacing it with the 6)
- Macbook Air
- iPhone 7 Plus
- DJI Osmo

Part Seven

Go ALL IN

This chapter is dedicated to the people who have raised their hand and shouted out "MEEEE!!! I'm ready to travel this world like a crazy nomad too!"
I salute you!
Full time travel or extended travel is not for everyone, but if you've read this far, I'm guessing it's for you.
If you're sitting there thinking "I don't really want to travel all the time, but I want to live differently than other people", then this chapter is something you should still read. I am including some key tips on living a more abundant and exciting life in here that you won't want to miss.

I'm going to go over all the nitty gritty details with you, so hold onto your knickers! I know how intimidating the thought of selling your house, all your stuff, and just jumping into a world of travel can be! It scared the living daylights out of me and my husband for weeks, but anything worth it is going to make your heart skip a beat.

We are going to cover topics like:
- The pros and cons of full time travel
- What to do about taxes, healthcare, insurance, and all other adulting requirements
- Geo arbitrage, meaning, how to leverage things like currency conversion or the cost of living in different countries to stretch your dollar WAY further than you ever thought
- Visas. How long you can visit countries, and other legal things you would want to know
- Tips on starting, as well as tips for actually living the nomadic lifestyle
- My personal stories and experiences on the road
- How to NOT full time travel, but live a crazy cool life anyway (Tiny homes, RV living, etc)

Being a full time digital nomad is freaking fantastic. I'm not going to hold that back! I truly believe it's one of the best life decisions I have ever made and I wish more people would dive into it as well. Most people will never even TRY this kind of a lifestyle, all because of fear. Letting fear hold them back and dictate their entire life.

That fear will ultimately keep them in a cubicle, taking orders from a boss they hate, and wishing life was different.
Life can be different.
YOU are the only thing that is stopping you from living the life you want. Just you.
Not your spouse, or kids, or job: ***you.***
I know it's much easier to say "well, I have 'x' responsibility, so I really can't live a different way of life", but it's not always true. Are there people with your same responsibilities living life in a way that you want to be? Sure there are! Which means you can too.
If you want it badly enough, you will make it happen.
There are of course many people who wouldn't actually want to be a digital nomad, and that is fine and dandy. I am a firm believer of 'each to their own' and I only want people to do things that align with their goals.
For me and my husband, that is the digital nomad lifestyle.

I have spent the last decade of my life trying to figure out how to make the digital nomad life work for me. Throughout my working career I've always CRAVED more freedom and those cravings seemed to intensify the more I tried to ignore them. At first I wrote the feelings off as some 'pre life crisis', you know, the one you get before the harsh reality of adulthood fully sets in. Everyone in their early 20's seemed to be jet setting around the world, and I didn't want to be left out. No matter how many trips I took, it never seemed to fill the urge to be on the road, which is how I knew I wasn't just looking for a vacation or sabbatical. I was looking for a blueprint that would allow me to live the life I was destined for.
After tons of research, I realized I would have to make some radical changes in my life in order to make working and living abroad viable. It's been said "Everything worth it hurts a little bit" and I am a firm believer in that being true. It's by no means EASY to live a life on the road, always traveling, always on the move; but it's the life I know I must live.

So is it all as good as it's cracked up to be?
Yes.
One million times YES.
It's a night and day comparison to being stuck in one town or one office you hate.

There is no way of me really putting it into perspective for you, you'll just have to try it and find out for yourself!
But if I had to try and give you a sneak peek of WHY it's so good, I guess I would explain it like this:

I wake up each morning, usually without an alarm, ready to face the day with a mixture of hard work, exploration and gratitude. The place that I wake up in has been carefully selected for one reason or another. Maybe it's a modern high rise condo in the downtown core of a bustling city, or perhaps it's a thatched roof villa in a humid jungle. Either way, I have picked the experience to be different from others I have had, so I can sample different ways of life across the globe. Each day I set aside time to work on my writing, blogs, social media accounts, emails, and other career building activities. I will perch myself up by a window, take my laptop down to a local cafe, or sometimes work in bed. With the remaining hours of the day, I try and take in local culture, try new foods, go for walks with Trevor, take photos, learn languages, read books, and plan my next adventure. I get to run multiple businesses with my husband, each revolving around our core values, and each with a lot of heart and soul pouring into them on a daily basis. There are days when I might work 12-16 hours straight, but somehow it doesn't seem as soul crushing when it's doing something I love, in a place that inspires me. There are other days when I might only do 1 hour of work in a day and spend the rest being a tourist, and those days always make incredible memories.
At night Trevor and I usually watch a movie or a documentary, or we head out to see our surroundings under the stars. We always set aside time that is just for us and has nothing to do with work.
It's not always glamorous, but it's my dream life.
If we find ourselves in an expensive city or country, we move. If we love the place we are in, we stay longer. If we want to share the experience with others, we invite friends.
I don't have a boss breathing down my neck, I don't have a morning commute filled with stress, and I don't have debt or bills piling up and making me feel hopeless. I have the most wonderful views, (usually) great weather, and a creative freedom based lifestyle.
I wouldn't change it for the world.

Do I still have insanely bad days? Of course I do! But I'm willing to take the good with the bad in order to live this way of life.

23- The Pro's and Con's

I get asked A LOT about the Pros and the Cons of being a digital nomad. There certainly are a lot of 'pros', but I want to be honest about the 'cons' as well. There are a lot of bloggers out there who make the travel life look like a fairytale 24/7, and that's really not the case! Before I get into the things that drive me mad, let's re-cap on some of the pros, as they are the reason I put up with this shit in the first place!

Pros:

Getting to see the world

Duh, right!? While this is one of the most obvious pros on the list, I wanted to point out why it means so much to me.
In the past I have found that visiting a place for a few days, feeling rushed and pressured to 'get it all in' during time off work, wasn't satisfying at all. Sure it was better than being at work, but I always felt like I needed a vacation from my vacation.
It was like I had entered some contest for packing the most crap into a week-long itinerary as possible, so I had a new activity for every hour of the day. It was exhausting, and usually meant I was doing weird touristy things I didn't even like.
With only one or two weeks' vacation given at work, that usually meant I was super limited to where I was going to spend my time off. It's too hard to book a 20 hour flight to Bali when travel time alone will shave 2 full days off the trip, so Florida and Mexico kept becoming regular spots.

Being a full time digital nomad I can SEE THE WORLD with no time limit, pressure, or restrictions. I can take my sweet ass time to travel to far-away lands, and even more time within the actual countries themselves. I'm not rushed and I can take my time to soak up all the culture I want.

I can keep making a mighty bucket list knowing I have the ability to follow through. I can dream and fantasize about new places to travel to, and then start making the itinerary!
Trust me, there is SO much of this world I want to see, it's really going to take me a few decades at least!

Meeting tons of friendly and interesting new people

Whenever someone tells a story about a past adventure, the people they encountered are usually a big part of the tale. Traveling to new places, I've had the privilege of meeting some remarkable people whom I will never forget. It's funny how some people will just stick to you. It might have been something wise they said that made an impression, or maybe it was something you watched them do, but I find many acquaintances still make an impact in the way I live my life. Traveling to different places and meeting the people who live there is always eye opening. They have different customs, cultures, languages, ideas, habits, and traditions. Taking the time to meet new friends and spend time with others add something to my life that is truly rich. We all have lessons to learn from each other.

Having more flexibility to visit long distance friends

My girlfriend, reporter and host Julie Stewart-Binks (AKA, JSB), is moving from Los Angeles to New York to dominate sports TV on a new coast. Knowing this, I carefully planned an extended layover in a few months so I can spend some quality face time with her in the Big Apple. I love being able to tweak my travel plans when I want to see someone I care about. Plus, I get to plop my homeless ass on her couch for a few days and have her show me around.

Tasting new foods

Any of my personal friends know I like to eat. No, scratch that, I LOVE to eat. I spend most of my day thinking about what I am going to eat next or devouring plates that are put down in front of me. My husband is exactly the same way!
Getting to add new flavours and dishes into my taste bud catalogue is one of the best things about traveling full time. It's always great to return to a place where I had previously discovered a new favourite food and getting to indulge in it all over again.

Feeling accomplished

There is something to be said about checking an item off my bucket list! It feels deeply satisfying! Have you ever written anything down on your to-do list, even if you already finished it, just so you could tick it off? Me too!
I'm not saying anything bad about the dreamers of the world, but I don't want to spend my whole life JUST dreaming. I want to dream it, and then DO it!
Traveling full time with my soul mate, hustling at my dream career, and still engaging in hobbies, makes me feel accomplished and proud.

Being the creative director of my career

I love being an entrepreneur. Better yet, I love being an entrepreneur on the road. Traveling while working gives me a rush of creativity that I can't get sitting in one spot. The world is my oyster! I've learned enough about business development throughout my different ventures that I feel totally capable of starting and succeeding with any type of work I want to do. All I need is Wi-Fi and the passion to pursue an idea with hunger and drive. That is a beautiful thing!

Having the ability to give back in person

Giving back to others is an amazing selfless act that I wish I had started sooner.

Giving back to others in person is a million times better! I want to know the people whose lives I am making an impact in, so I can truly understand the power of paying it forward. It can be as small as overtipping someone who deserves it, or on a bigger scale like offering my skills or time to a person in need. Either way, it gives me a lot of joy when I can see the power of a good deed first hand.

Living in tons of different houses

I love houses, especially unique ones! One of the best things about living a nomadic lifestyle is picking out where to live next! I love mixing it up! I can go from busy city to quiet beach town, from super modern to old and rustic. I've stayed in buildings that were centuries old with hidden nooks and crannies everywhere and I've stayed in brand new apartments with state of the art technology. It's fun to sample all the different types of housing and ways of life. I love being able to pick a small rancher bungalow and then switch it up to a warehouse loft. Sometimes I have a garden and other times it's a stone wall courtyard. An elevator might take me to the top floor, or I might even be living in an RV. My love for houses is what got me interested in real estate in the first place, so that obsession will never go away! Instead of having to pick one home to spend the rest of my life in (and trying to make it perfect) I can live in all the different types of houses I have ever dreamed of.
Plus I have to admit that moving out before something breaks or needs a crazy deep clean is such a perk!

Constantly learning new things

Traveling has taught me things I never would have learned otherwise! Every single day is a new lesson in some aspect.

<u>Sense of Direction:</u> I have to learn about distances, street names, and the layouts of cities. This also includes how to find my bearings and take account of landmarks to help guide me through unfamiliar places.

I continue to learn more and more about this massive Earth we are on, as I am always researching airports and cities to fly into. I still have those moments of "Oh, I didn't know this city was in this country!"

Languages: I have a secret desire to be a full time polyglot, spending my days studying and speaking multiple languages. For now, I'm happy just to learn, "Where's the bathroom!?" in different tongues. I speak English and Spanish, with an embarrassingly beginners grasp on French. I've taken Italian lessons (something I want to continue with) and in addition to these languages, I would love to be able to speak: Portuguese, Romanian, Russian and Korean. Just being around people and listening to them speak makes me happy. I love picking up words here and there, and in all honesty, it helps me understand English that much more!

Customs and Traditions: Growing up in Canada, I did experience a lack of culture and customs. (Don't freak out fellow Canucks, just hear me out!) Sure there is hockey, maple syrup, Tim Hortons, and poutine… but since the country is so young and so multicultural, it doesn't have a lot of age old traditions. I feel this is why I love learning about the culture of the country I am in. Whether it be art, dance, ceremonies, religion, holidays or even superstition, I find it all fascinating! Getting to see these things first hand is so fulfilling and magical!

Filling in the gaps: Have you ever read a book and they used a word or talked about something that was so foreign to your mind that you kind of just skipped over it? I've had plenty of those moments, but I have found while traveling, some of those gaps get delightfully filled in! I will all of a sudden be faced with something that was once such a mystery and have an, 'Oh THAT'S what they meant!' moment. It's kind of like putting together a lifelong mystery jigsaw puzzle and starting to see the picture more clearly.

About myself: I'm always learning new things about myself as a person while being a digital nomad, and that is a great thing.
The more unique circumstances I put myself in, the more I am forced to step up as a leader in my own life. It's been a wonderful soul searching event so far, but I feel as if I have just tapped the surface.

The flexibility of being able to come and go as I please

Getting to see the world really covered this topic as well, but there is so much more to it than just travel. A friend once told me a story about a job he suffered through for YEARS where he actually had to ask to go to the bathroom. It wasn't like he was an air traffic controller or anything, and people's lives were not on the line, but he has this belittling task of asking permission each time nature called. He said he put up with it for so long because he was vying for a promotion, which he never ended up getting, and actually got laid off instead! *Quel Nightmare!* Being a digital nomad and my own boss means I don't have to put up with any of that crap and I can come and go as I please. If I want to leave a country, I do. If I want to take the day off, I do. If I want to jump in a bathtub full of jellybeans while listening to The Cure, I will! I can change my mind, adapt, switch direction and even multitask on passion projects. Living within my own set of rules is powerful and freeing at the same time.

Have you ever seen a super cheap anomaly flight sale on Facebook and thought "omg...like this is SO cheap! I can't believe it! I have to find a way to go on this trip!"...but then you never do because you couldn't get time off, etc.
I don't have to deal with that anymore. If there is a crazy first class flight or luxury hotel on sale and the dates are all weird, good! I will 100% take advantage of it because I can!

It all boils down to CHOICE and FREEDOM. I think the biggest pros of a digital nomad lifestyle revolve around those two words.

Cons:

It's not all rainbows and sunshine folks!

There are many times when I can't find a place to wash my extremely smelly clothing, or my flights been delayed for the millionth time, or a dead cockroach just appeared beside my plate in a shady restaurant.

Being forced to be uncomfortable

There are days when I have not wanted to feel uncomfortable, but that was just too damn bad!
Being on the road all the time means constant new environments and that can get super uncomfortable! This might mean trying to talk to someone in a language I don't understand, being completely effing lost with no way to recalibrate, having to eat weird food that may or may not contain dog meat, or as simple as just not feeling quite right. I'm always being forced to leave my comfort zone, and while that is good for me long term, it can feel like hell in the process.

Not always having things I want (brands, foods, etc)

Traveling all the time and to different countries means brands and products available are always changing. And sometimes that drives me mental. I have actually had legit temper tantrums over not being able to find contact solution or face wipes. (I know, not very minimalist, but extremely high maintenance of me, right?)
Any guys reading this may or may not understand the complete and utter devastation most girls go through when we can't get our necessities. I'm not the most high maintenance woman that ever lived, but I am sure as hell not the lowest maintenance either!

Okay, as an example, we were on the coast of Ecuador and we had just hired a driver to take us over an hour to the nearest grocery store so we could stock up. They had carbs, carbs, carbs, more carbs, foreign fruits I couldn't identify, and more carbs.
I'm not a chef, so I'm usually looking for some healthy meals I can buy and take home with little prep work, but that concept had not hit Ecuador yet. There was no almond milk, no Skinny Pop, nothing I was used to. Combine that with not being able to find mascara, body wash, sensitive toothpaste or a charger for my laptop that had just broken, I had a meltdown in the middle of the store. Not my proudest moment!

Not being able to find foods you want, makeup you want, or basic personal care items you actually NEED is maddening. I'm not sure if anything bothers me as much as this, even though you'd think I would be getting used to it!

Travel insurance becomes quite the expense

Travel insurance is a MUST for us! 100%, non-negotiable, written in stone, no getting around it. That translates to a chunk of the budget being spent on it! There are lots of bills I no longer have (like utility, property taxes, cable, etc) but travel insurance can add up. We will spend between $1200-$1800 CAD on travel insurance per year.

Going over budget ALL the time

Talking about expenses, traveling full time is like a boxing match with my bank account, to which I am always the loser. No matter how much I plan, research or sacrifice, I am invariably going to surpass my budget. I've read blogs about travelers who have managed to stay under budget consistently over months or years at a time and I'm starting to think its all part of a big prank to fool me.
It kind of comes at me from all angles. Traveling constantly makes me go over budget, running my own business makes me go over budget, and just opening my eyes every morning seems to make me go over budget as well. It's not that I am walking down the street and I see a scooter made out of pure gold and just can't restrain myself from buying it; it's the little things adding up that kick my budgets ass into the ground.
Bottles of water here, forgotten power converter there, with a side of "crap I totally forgot this city has 18% VAT on hotel rooms". I will admit there are times when I sabotage the budget from my own gluttony or laziness, like the time I paid for an extra night at a hotel so I could have a mid-day nap (oops!), but they are not the main killers. The last thing I want to do is get myself back into a pickle with credit card debt, or spending more than I earn.

Tasting new foods

Funny how a pro can quickly become a con! While getting to indulge in new food is one of my favourite things to do, it can also be horrifying! I've found myself sitting in a restaurant, dying of hunger and staring at a menu I can't understand, but ordering anyway. Then some indescribable blob of food is put in front of me that actually tastes dreadfully more repulsive than it looks. Lunch FAIL! There are times when I am not in the mood to play 'guess that dish' and I just want to eat something remotely familiar, but sadly it's not always possible.

Feeling guilty

I've felt guilt in many ways because of my nomadic lifestyle and it's something I am still working on to this day.
I feel guilty for not putting in enough facetime with my amazing friends, not seeing my siblings or aging parents, and for not physically being there for people I care about. Many of the people close to me don't understand that being a digital nomad isn't just 'for fun' and that it encompasses my career and how I support myself. For many, a glance into my life just looks like I am messing around, playing online and being fickle, which can cause some tension in relationships. I want to be there for all of the important people in my life, but I can't put my own on hold in order to do it. This has me in a constant back and forth with myself on what the 'right' thing is to do. It's not easy and the guilt comes with an overbearing weight.

There is also guilt about the things I see while on the road. I encounter a lot of poverty and it feels dirty to turn a blind eye.
Here I am, gallivanting past people who don't even have enough money to feed their kids, and my only worry is the Wi-Fi password. Trevor and I make it a priority to give back to the communities that we visit, but it never seems enough. There are times when I wish I could just give everything we have, but I know it still won't make the impact that is needed. I have had many sleepless nights with the guilt of privilege keeping me awake.

Luggage

UGH. I could just have a fit talking about this right now. I wish I could place all my things in a little cute backpack and skip into the sunset without a care in the world. Well, I can't. Not even close!

DUFL, a company that holds most of my outfits and ships them to me, has helped SO much with this, but I still struggle.

My luggage is always an issue somehow. When I had two little bags, I was only allowed one, or I thought I should get down to one to make life easier. Then when I had one bag, train travel proved that I should have two small ones to be able to keep them near me. But then two is harder to walk with in busy areas. But then one sucks for international flights because what if it's lost and I have no backup carryon….. and this goes on and on and on.

It gets broken, it gets lost, it's overweight, it's the biggest pain in the ass to get up 6 flights of stairs.

What I need is luggage that carries itself, is never weighed, always reaches its destination and is cute. Anyone make something like that!? I am currently in the market for some better luggage and I have been researching for months about what kind I should go with. I currently have 1 big ass checked bag called 'Frank'. Frank sure does hold a lot, but he's bulky and impossible to travel with by train or small plane. I'm thinking of returning back to 1 medium sized checked and 1 carryon. Wish me luck!

Power Outages (and other third world problems)

Power outages, internet service issues, and more serious things like tropical storms, can really take the bounce out of my step. (Especially when my business is involved)

We once rented a beach house in Latin America without first checking a few vital things. MOST Latin American stoves run on propane with gravity flush toilets, so we didn't even think to check. Bad move! El Niño was raging his ugly head and we had constant power outages that caused some major discomfort. Our toilets used an electric pump, our stove was electric (like the only electric stove on the continent) and this meant no cooking, showering, flushing the toilet or other basic necessities when the power was out. Which was a lot. (I won't even go into the Wi-Fi being out for days and days and having no way to reach friends, family, or anything to do with our business, costing us hundreds if not thousands of dollars). We got a little tired of eating stale crackers and playing cards by candlelight.

Ironically most beautiful, warm weather places in the world are also the same places that have fierce storms and subpar infrastructures. When we used to see a gorgeous tropical hut we'd say "book it!", but now we say "what are the hookups, backup plans, systems and amenities like!?"

The paperwork

Yawn. I became a digital nomad to get away from so many bureaucratic formalities, not to add to it! Paperwork dealing with entry visas, customs declarations, insurances and other travel related documents is just plain annoying.

The long travel days

I wish I could fly to every destination direct, and in a first class lie flat bed, but some wishes will never come true. We have a budget that we need to make an attempt to stick to, otherwise we'll be forced to go home forever, and that means getting creative on travel days. I will have to stick in an extra layover, or book us on the red-eye, all in an effort to make traveling more affordable. Sometimes I have us on some wild goose chase through more airport terminals than you can imagine, and after a 36 hour travel day, we are both cranky AF! It's hard to be patient when I haven't slept or showered in 2 days. These long travel days usually end in me snapping at someone for the smallest thing, like not putting a lemon wedge in my water.

Trying to stay productive

I still haven't completely ditched the whole "Whoooo hoooo I'm on vacation!" mindset when I land in a new place. My heart and soul just want to go into vacation mode, but my bank account says I have to get to work! Confining myself to stay focused and productive on tasks when I just really want to play is bloody hard! I kind of go through these motions like binge eating an entire tub of ice-cream. I will be all "carpe diem bitches!" and then through guilt and shame I will strap myself in and get some work done.

I'm not sure I will ever have the answer for this predicament. All I can do is try! I will forever be on this rollercoaster of wanting to be a responsible business owner and a carefree wanderlust tourist. *Le sigh*.

Jet lag

It's real y'all! They say it takes a day to recover for each time zone you pass through, and I believe it. We usually try and stay in a particular time zone for 1-3 months, but more frequent travel can leave us with a certain malaise. I don't know how international business people do it! They fly around the world several times a week.

Trying to explain my life or work to others

When people ask me "Where do you live?" or "What do you do?" there are times when I want to answer with "I'm a waitress from Florida" because it would be much easier than the 45 minute conversation that is about to follow. Don't get me wrong, I actually LOVE talking to people about my lifestyle, but sometimes it feels like a record on repeat. We live in a world where a particular way of life has become so engrained on its citizens that many people are unwilling to accept the idea there might be several ways to skin a cat. I get a lot of 'tsk tsk tsk's' from anyone born before 1960 when they find out I'm a childless vagabond who works on the internet.

Not having a sense of stability

People ask me this all the time, "Don't you miss having a home? You know, a place that you know, that is your safe zone, where everything is familiar and comfortable?"
Yes.

If I had all the money in the world, I would buy a house and fill it up with my favourite things and know it was there waiting for me. But I don't have all the money in the world, so something's gotta give. That something is me trading in familiar comforts for a life of travel and adventure, but that doesn't mean I don't miss the old way of life. Sometimes I just want to sit on a certain couch, in a certain outfit, surrounded by certain people, eating a certain meal, and watching a certain show; but that doesn't happen very often.

I think the cons can be summarized into missing loved ones, not having a sense of normalcy and having to be uncomfortable more than I would like!

24 -Become a Digital Nomad

In order to be a true digital nomad, you need to have your income streams nailed down. Work your little buns off until your income is at a high enough rate that you can support yourself in your goal atmosphere. There is no point of going into debt halfway around the world, and being forced to come home just to start from scratch.

In the EARN section of this book, I went over many different ways you can make a living online and remotely, so your best bet is to establish a career in one of those fields. The best kind of job you can have as a full time traveler is one that only requires Wi-Fi.
If you skimmed past that section, it might be a good idea to revisit it before you start planning out your next year long travel adventure. There is a chance you're still unsure of exactly WHAT you could do for a career on the road, and that is where I think having a mentor is important. Talk to someone who has already gone through the steps of setting up a remote business, because they will have valuable hands on advice for you.
There may be dozens of good opportunities for you, but you might not be able to identify them without the help of an experienced entrepreneur.

Affording nomadic life

So just how much money are you going to need?

That will depend on what kind of a traveler you are! One thing is going to make all the difference in the world to you and that is something called 'Geoarbitrage'.

If you have read Tim Ferris's "Four Hour Work Week", you're likely already familiar with this concept. To give you a definition, it's the act of paying much less for the exact same quality of goods or services by leveraging cost of living and currency exchanges. To put it as simply as I can: It's paying $2 for a homemade vegetable noodle bowl on a lush garden patio in Vietnam instead of $18 for the same noodle bowl out of a crowded LA eatery. Or another example: It's like spending $1000/m on a 600 sq ft beach front hotel room in Bali that includes daily massages and breakfast; compared to spending $1000/m on a 200sq ft rundown studio apartment in New York City.

You take your money where it stretches the farthest, therefore allowing you to do more with less! If you can live in a country where your income only needs to be $400 a week to live like a king, it puts way less pressure on transitioning from the corporate world into your new entrepreneur life.

A great tool to find out what country you can practice Geoarbitrage in, is the website numbeo.com. You can put in the city you are looking to travel to or live in, and it gives you the cost of things from wine to housing to cinema tickets, in whatever currency you want. I find most things are absolutely accurate, with the exception being on housing/rental prices (which are much too low on Numbeo).

Get your googling on and find out where your currency is going gangbusters right now. The more your dollar is up over the country in question, the farther each cent will stretch!

Another point on money. Have some before you go!
When I first became full location independent, it was after having a track record of consistent income. I didn't just pack my bags and take off into the sunset when I made my first $5. I tested myself, the markets, and took time to see if I would encounter big fluctuations in income (which I did, and still do!) Being your own boss is the best thing on this planet, but it's also the most unpredictable thing. Give it some time to see how your income flow works and start to put some cash away into savings.

Where to find your home abroad

How much of a deal you can score on accommodation will usually be determined by how long you are staying. I do find Numbeo is very LOW on the pricing scale, as I believe they are using local data, and we all know locals live for much less than tourists.

For example, I was researching how much an Edinburgh apartment would be for the month. On Numbeo it says a 1 bedroom apartment in the city centre is about £800, yet I couldn't find anything less than £1500 pounds on Airbnb. A local wouldn't be using Airbnb though, they would be going through the normal rental channels and perhaps even signing a 6-12 month lease. If you know you are going to stay in a location for 3 months or more, try going through local rental boards and agencies to pay a more realistic price!

Each city and country has their own sites and processes, so I can't fill in this blank for you, but just google things like you were a local and figure it out.

As for the major sites, we usually use:
- Homeaway
- Air BnB
- We also check hotels on hotelscombined.com. In some countries (like Thailand, Vietnam, and Indonesia) a nice hotel can be the same price as a short term rental. We've found pretty posh, 3 to 4 star, well rated hotels in those areas for $25 USD a night! (Which would be $750/m to live in a pretty swanky hotel!)

If you have a particular skill, like caring for horses or agriculture, there are many opportunities to housesit and have your accommodations paid for. There are sites that help to connect you with homeowners looking to get away, that need a little extra help keeping their home in running order. They aren't looking for freeloaders to water a few houseplants, usually the tasks are things like keeping elaborate gardens alive, caring for livestock, and if you're lucky, walking and befriending their family pooch!

Negotiating

If you want to rent something on Homeaway or AirBnB that is over 2 weeks in duration, ALWAYS negotiate!
Owners don't like wear and tear on their rentals, and that is exactly what happens when they have turn over every few days. Having 1 or 2 responsible people in a rental for a few months means less cost in cleaning and property management and less wear and tear. We once rented a 3 bedroom house for 2 months and because it slept 6, but there were only 2 of us, we negotiated $300/m off the rent. Less occupant's means less water consumption, less utilities and again, less wear on the property.
If I see a property I like, but the price seems way higher than other comparable rentals, I will still contact them and try and negotiate. One time we splurged on this incredible ocean front condo in Nuevo Vallarta, Mexico that was listed at $550/night for $4000 for the entire month! The owner never updated his listing to reflect monthly rental pricing, so it was on Airbnb as $16,500 for the whole month, which seemed WACKO! After messaging him, we were able to negotiate that down to $4000, which is still a high amount, but this gem was worth every penny!

Staying Longer than 1 or 2 months

You might find a sweet deal if you are willing to sign a lease for 3 to 6 months, but I would advise against it, unless you know the property or area well. There are so many things a listing can't tell you that you will soon find out in person. Maybe the front room gets so hot during the day it's unbearable, or maybe the neighbours are hardcore party animals. I like to commit to a few weeks in a place, leaving the possibility of extending once I have experienced what the property is really like!
I usually like to stay a max of 3 months in any certain rental or spot.

Be Flexible

Sometimes moving locations half way through a stay, or modifying the dates slightly will make all the difference. I was looking in Miami for this winter and I just put in Jan 1 to March 1, and guess what, not a whole lot was left!

There was a whole bunch of overpriced, and bottom of the barrel places left. BUT, when I looked into getting 1 place for just January, and another place for February, a ton more rentals opened up. This is because some vacation homes on the market might have been taken for only ONE week in mid Feb, taking it out of my search results all together. When I cut the trip into 2 parts, more variety of properties became available. Same thing happened when I started looking Jan 5th instead of Jan 1st. Everyone and their dog apparently rented a condo in Miami over New Year's, so it was skewing my results. Play around with dates, lengths of time, and switching properties to find the sweet deals on longer term rentals.

Rental Checklist

My checklist might not be the same as yours, but over the years I have learned what to ask and what to look for in a home if I want to be comfortable. Here is my cheat sheet:

- ✓ Is there a restaurant, convenience or grocery store within a 10 minute walk?
- ✓ Is there fast, reliable internet? Can they do a speed test and send it to me?
- ✓ Is the stove propane, gas or electric?
- ✓ Is there a microwave?
- ✓ Is there a dishwasher, washer, dryer? If not, is there an iron and clothes hanger?
- ✓ What floor is it on?
- ✓ Is there private outdoor space?
- ✓ Are there ceiling fans, air con, etc?
- ✓ What are the past reviews saying about the rental? Have any past problems been fixed? If there are no past reviews, ask them WHY!
- ✓ Where are the nearest public transportation stops?
- ✓ Are visitors allowed without extra charge?
- ✓ What is the cancellation policy?
- ✓ What is the deposit amount?
- ✓ What is the area like in terms of safety?
- ✓ Is housekeeping available? At what cost?

The Rest of Your Budget

Flights into a country and accommodation will usually make up over 50% of your living expenses. In order to figure out the rest of your expat budget, take these things into consideration:

Food
Research on Numbeo the cost for:
- A basic local lunch
- A brand name fast food meal (if that's your weakness)
- A mid-range dinner
- A super luxe, let's get it on, fine dining experience
- Grocery staples (like milk, water, bread, cheese, butter, veggies, fruits, meats)
- Booze

It's a good idea to get an estimate on how many meals per month you will be eating/making at home, versus how many you will dine out for. In Southeast Asia, you can eat lunch at a restaurant for cheaper than you can cook at home, but for some European countries lunch will eat up a weeks' worth of grocery budget. Some countries that have heavy restrictions or taxations on alcohol might shock you with atrocious prices for bottles of wine, while others may surprise you with $0.30 beer. Know these things, and your own habits and preferences, before being blind-sided by them.

Transportation
You will want to check out local public transportation, cost and ease of taxi's, and maybe even renting your own car. If you were able to score a rental unit that is walking distance from everything, transportation will be less important, thus freeing up a section of your budget.

Attractions and Fun
As crazy as it seems, it's actually all too easy to get into old routines while living abroad. You need to make sure you are still touring and sightseeing to make all those miles travelled worthwhile.
Look ahead as best you can and try and plan 1 attraction or fun excursion per week. There are many free things you can do (like hiking or museums) so take those into account as well. Make a 'fun' section of your budget and stick to it!

Connectivity

Whether you are using TEP, a local SIM card in an unlocked phone, or local internet cafes, it's best to budget out the cost of internet, as you may find yourself using it more than you originally thought. I also put in a small amount for Skype calls, Wi-Fi on flights, using a hotels phone, etc.

Human Stuff

You know, all the things we buy. For girls that might be makeup, face wash, and getting our roots done. For guys that might be razors, shave gel, and haircuts. You know what you need and what you buy, so track it for a month and figure it out. Think if you'll need that particular item IN the country you want to go to. Example is a hair straightener for me. If we are in a crazy humid country, there is no way my flat iron is going to do diddly squat on my wavy hair, so I don't need it.

If you are going somewhere really remote, make sure all your stuff is in good working order. I learned this the hard way when I KNEW my 2010 MacBook Pro charger was almost dead, but I brought it anyway. It was frayed and had the wires showing, you know, real safe stuff. Anyway, it totally died midway through our super remote Ecuador stay, and guess what? Finding its replacement was nearly impossible. I had to hire a 'fixer' that drove to Quito and Guayquil to find one, and it ended up costing me $220.

Bring good condition essentials with you and know what your replacement cost situation looks like.

Emergency Fund

You will dip into this fund all the time for things that aren't even close to being an emergency, but that is just the way long term travel works! You need one anyway. How much? It's different for everyone, but just have a reserve that can carry you for a few months if need be.

With these tips, you can make yourself a pretty well rounded budget, which will help you to discover what countries you can afford to live in with the income you are currently making. If your business takes an upswing, you can upgrade your situation. If your income drops significantly, you will have an idea of where you can cut costs.

WORKBOOK 20

I wanted to give you an example of all the things you can research on Numbeo (or any other cost of living data site out there)
For this example, I collected info on two very popular, yet different, tourist destinations. I also left a blank column so you can look up your own bucket list destination and pop the numbers in to compare. All figures are in USD just to make life easier.

	Barcelona, Spain	Denpasar, Bali	
Meal (inexpensive restaurant)	$11.60	$1.85	
Dinner for 2, mid range	$46.41	$14.80	
Fast Food combo	$8.12	$3.70	
Local beer	$3.48	$2.41	
Cappuccino	$1.99	$2.02	
Coke	$2.08	$1.01	
Water	$1.34	$0.46	
Milk	$0.93	$1.42	
Bread	$1.48	$0.92	
Eggs	$2.26	$1.23	
Chicken (1kg)	$7.19	$3.20	
Apples (1kg)	$2.17	$2.12	
Bottle of Wine (local, mid)	$5.80	$24.06	
1 ticket, local transport	$2.49	$0.37	
1 ticket, cinema	$9.86	$3.70	
1 bedroom apartment	$987.01	$120.33	
3 bedroom apartment	$1,613.06	$227.00	

Look at how much lower Bali is on things like transportation, rent, and dining out. But check out the price of WINE! Wayyyyy higher than Barcelona!

Research a city you want to go to on Numbeo and fill in the values.

Printable & Editable Version at traveloffpath.com/workbooks

Adulting on the road

How long can you stay?

I could make a whole book on this topic alone, but I will spare you the sleep inducing details. Each country has its own rules and regulations about how long a visitor can stay. A 'visitors or tourist visa' is usually issued automatically upon entry to many major countries you will enter (like Mexico for example) without you having to do anything extra at all. You just put your butt on the plane, fill out your little form along with your customs card, and you get stamped upon entry at the customs desk. Mexico is a country that automatically gives Canadians a 6 month tourist visa, meaning I can stay and be a tourist for 180 days without breaking any laws. If I want to stay longer, I will have to formally apply. (Which is what I should have done all those years ago when I may or may not have been deported)
Some countries want you to apply beforehand, or instruct you to fill out certain papers upon arrival. The lengths of tourist visas that are issued can range from 72 hours, right up to 360 days!
When we went to Ecuador for 6 months, we had to apply while we were still in Canada to extend our tourist visa from 3 months, to 6 months. There was paperwork, meeting with the consulate in Vancouver, giving them proof we could support ourselves with bank statements, a police check and application fee.

American and Canadian passports have just about the same tourist visa requirements for popular destinations, so I'm just going to list some as of 2017 in Canada. Here is basic list of tourist visas for different countries (with extensions usually possible)

Countries you can stay for 90 days:
- Argentina
- Australia
- Croatia
- Dominican Republic
- Ecuador
- El Salvador
- France
- Germany

- Ireland
- Italy
- Jamaica
- Japan
- Malta
- Morocco
- New Zealand
- Nicaragua
- Portugal
- Romania
- Slovenia
- Spain
- Sweden
- Switzerland
- Turkey
- Uruguay

Want to stay somewhere longer without the burden and cost of extended visas? Check these out;

Countries you can stay for 180 days:
- Antigua & Barbuda
- Bahamas (8 months!)
- Barbados
- Columbia
- Georgia (360 days!)
- South Korea
- Mexico
- Peru
- St.Kitts
- United States
- United Kingdom

Here were some that surprised me at first, but some can be extended online-

Countries you can stay for 30 days:
- Indonesia
- Laos
- Lebanon

- Maldives
- Philippines
- Qatar
- Saint Lucia
- Sri Lanka
- Thailand
- Vietnam

I used Wikipedia for this info, so please do your own research if seriously considering staying in a country.

What you need to know about a country

Other than budget and visas, there are a few other things you should be savvy on before you decide to reside in a particular country.

Basic phrases

English is SO widely spoken these days, but it's not something that you should rely on. I have found myself in many circumstances where I had no phone battery left for google translate and someone in front of me who couldn't understand a word I was saying.

I would write down (or memorize) these following words/phrases:
Hello
Thank you
Where is…
How much
Yes
No
Please
Water
Bathroom
I don't understand
1, 5, 10, 100

If you want to get all fancy, try these longer phrases:

Where is the Bathroom?
What is this?
How much is that?
I would like to order…
How can I get to?
Can you help me?
Can you call me a taxi?
The bill/check, please!
That is too much!
I only want to pay…
One bottle of water please!
My name is…
What is your name?

Practice pronouncing some of these basic phrases (just watch youtube videos!) and keep a copy in your wallet just in case you might need them!

Weather & Seasons

In order to pack like a pro and know what climate you're in for, do some research on the seasonal weather and if there are major storms due to take place while you're there. Lots of popular destinations have seasons for hurricanes, typhoons, and other dangerous acts of nature you will want to be prepared for.

How you can get OUT of the country

Seems like a weird tip, right? Of course you know how to get out of the country! Probably the same way you came IN, by plane, train, bus, car or boat. But if you anything like me, I like to book one way tickets and plan my next destination as I go.

This isn't always the best way, because I have found myself 'stuck' in a country in relation to how much I WANT to spend to get out of it. What if the flights out of that country are double the cost of what you paid to fly in? Or what if there are no easy or cheap flights from that city to your next destination? You should take your exit strategy into consideration before you go.

The Voltage

For MANY destinations you will need some power adaptors and maybe even a converter! Find out what voltage and plugs your goal destination has and buy the adaptors before you go. They price them 500% higher at the airport to take advantage of forgetful travelers.

The Laws

If you want to spend a considerable amount of time in a country, especially 'living like a local', you will want to check out their laws. We have all seen tourists being jailed for speaking their mind, possessing a small amount of drugs that are considered legal in their own country, or even because of their sexual preference. When in doubt, google your heart out to make sure your lifestyle doesn't conflict with any strict laws that might be in place.

Your Life Back Home

Your Home

If you want to follow my template, that means you are going to sell your house or give up your rental and just go full out nomad! If you want to keep your home, you will want to rent it out to someone with a lease and a property manager in place to make it financially viable. Property managers cost money but are worth it in the long run to deal with the tenants while you are away.

Selling
Coming from the mouth of an ex-Realtor, use a professional to sell your house. Yes, they take a commission, but it's worth it in the end. It's their JOB to get you the highest possible price for your home, with the least amount of inconvenience. They will have photos taken, schedule appointments, host open houses, negotiate with buyers, and ensure you are happy with the deal. I've tried selling houses on my own, and even though I am experienced enough to do so, I still use a Realtor.
Have a few different Realtors come through your home and give you estimates on what they believe it will sell for and what their fees are. Call your bank and find out exactly how much is left owning on your mortgage and if there are any early pay off penalties. (Which make me want to scream by the way! Urgghhh banks!)
Then you can calculate based on the estimate of a sales price how much you will have left after fees, penalties and lawyer costs.

With the net income from your house (and all the crap in it) you will want to pay off any outstanding debts first and foremost.
Debt is a party pooper when you are traveling around the world. It eats into your monthly budget and causes tons of unnecessary stress. In fact, I really don't think anyone should be a digital nomad if they have any debt, even if their business is doing well.
Take the equity and demolish all debts.

Next, if there is anything left over, stash it away in savings. If you remember from past chapters, I have multiple savings accounts to help organize and dog-ear different moneys.

Giving up your rental
Letting go of your rental is much faster and easier than selling a house! Take into consideration how much you normally spend on rent, utilities and any other costs associated with you rental, and think about how you can transfer that budget into traveling full time.
If your income will be the same, the budget can stay the same and just morph into paying for different kinds of rentals in different countries.

If your income will be much lower, then what you used to spend on rent might not work with your new lifestyle. Time to get creative about how you will make up the difference!

Mail

Mail is a tough one! I still get important things in the mail to this day, no matter how many e-bills I have signed up for. There is no point in missing some urgent or sensitive piece of mail from the government or a bill collector and getting yourself in hot water, so having a system that will still collect and filter mail is key.

First Step: Give the government, all services and bills, your email address and make sure they have your permission to actually send you an email. Sign into any account you can think of (look through the cards in your wallet and past mail for the year to not miss anything) and select 'email correspondence' as your preferred method of contact.

Second Step: Get a UPS box. We pay about $150/y for a postal box that will collect our mail and parcels, unlimited, until we return. I love that they are a smaller local store and that I can even CALL them and ask them what might be there for me. (Example: "Hey! Is there a scary looking tax bill there for me?" Or "Did Amazon drop off a package?") If something is really life or death important, UPS will forward that mail to wherever I am in the world. Caveat to that is they have to send it air mail, so it's about the same price as a bottle of Dom P, but hey, what can you do. They also gave me an actual STREET address instead of a 'postal box' address, which is much easier to work with. I sleep much better at night knowing I have a system to safeguard this area of my life.

Your Cell Phone

If you are traveling for 30 days, sure, keep your phone on and go nuts, but if you are thinking of being gone for 3 months or more, you might want to switch it to 'vacation disconnect'.
If you are European or American, listen up: As Canadians, Trevor and I pay about $230/m for our cell phones with data. SICK RIGHT!

Canadian cell phone data is apparently made with diamonds, so there is no WAY I would keep my plan running while I am out of the country. We put it on 'vacation disconnect', which allows us to keep our same phone numbers and only charges us $10/m. Our actual PHONE still works, in the sense that we connect it to Wi-Fi and use Skype to call people if we need to.

I know many cell phone companies allow you to use your plan's data and minutes in a foreign country for small daily charges, but that can really add up!

We use TEP Wireless for traveling instead of expensive cellphone plans. It's a small device that works as a hotspot. We connect 5 devices at once (so both our phones and laptops), receive unlimited data, and it's only $8 per day when we choose to use it. If we have great hotel Wi-Fi, great, then we don't turn TEP on. When we run into long travel days, bad hotel or airport Wi-Fi, or just want to be connected no matter where we are, we turn it on! It's saved our asses more times than I can explain. I sincerely refuse to travel anywhere without bringing it with me.

My business and my sanity depend on it.

Your Credit Cards and Passport

Before you leave home, make sure your credit cards are not going to expire ANYTIME near your expected arrival back into your country. Getting replacement credit cards in isolated countries is a huge pain in the rear end!

Same thing goes for your passport. Most countries won't even grant you entry if you have less than 8 months left before your passport expires.

As a rule of thumb, I aim to have at least 5 years on my passport and 1 year on my credit cards.

Taxes

I'm not going to go into detail with taxes because I'm not an expert and you should consult one of them before hitting the road, however, some countries may have tax breaks if you don't return home for a while.

Example: if you are out globetrotting and not earning income from your home country, and you don't return for 2 years, you may have some tax breaks on that income come filing time. Best thing you can do is talk to an accountant who specializes in international taxes.

Another tip, do your taxes before you go on a big trip. Or else they will pile up. And you will start to cry. Not like I would know…

The Rest Of Your Crap

If you sold your house and most of your stuff to dive into this world lifestyle, you might still have some important things left over. Keepsakes, photos, clothing you can't shove into your suitcase, things like that.

The first few years I made the mistake of paying $170/m for a storage unit to house a few boxes of my stuff, which honestly equals out to more than I want to think about. Don't make that same mistake. Here is what you do:

Step One: Sell everything you can! We've gone over this enough times already, but even if you think you need or want it, you don't. Sell!

Step Two: Take your 1 or 2 small boxes with the items you literally could not part with and have a family member or a friend hold them for you. Bribe them with promises to bring them back cool souvenirs for the 2 sq ft of space you are borrowing from them.

Step Three: Get DUFL. I don't know a human being that can pack clothes for every possible scenario and climate into one suitcase. I also don't know anyone who would want to spend money on a flight home just to grab a different outfit. For this reason, DUFL is the best thing that has ever happened to us nomads.

I've explained it before, but here is the gist: You send them 90% of your clothing, they clean it, take pictures of it, and put it into a nice looking app for you.

Then when you want a change of outfits, clothes for a different type of climate, or just to rotate what you have been wearing, you place an order. They fold it and make it look like Christmas, place it into luggage, and it arrives at your hotel or rental in 1-3 days! Then you can send those same clothes back, or the old smelly ones you have been wearing for months, whatever floats your boat. It's a closet in the cloud and a way to get around having a dingy storage unit. It only costs $10 a month for them to hold unlimited clothing, shoes, and even surf boards or golf clubs for you. The shipment cost will depend on where you are, but I find it's still saving me money because I avoid checked bag fees, dry cleaning, and storage rentals.

Safety

I never realized how important safety was until I had a machete waving madly in my face, watching a gun being pressed to the back of my friends head.

It was near San Juan Del Sur in Nicaragua and our dream vacation just turned into a nightmare. Before I get into what happened, I just want to highlight how horribly irresponsible and ignorant our behaviour was. We were basically parading around without a care in the world and very apparently not worried about what was going on around us.

A group of friends and I rented a hilltop villa for 10 days and on our second last day we wanted some beach time! My sister and her boyfriend decided on a different activity that day, but we planned to meet at sunset for a dinner cruise.

Early in the day, we all packed up our cameras, phones (to text my sister), credit cards and passports (you need to show ID when exchanging money at the bank) and other valuable items and headed off to a remote beach. We wanted a place where we could lounge around all day with no one else in sight, and we sure found it! After hours of snapping pics, laughing and lounging the day away, our day turned into a nightmare.

From the jungle, two men with bandanas across their faces came running from the trees, shouting and waving something in their arms. At first I thought it was kids playing a game, but as they got closer I realized just how serious the situation had become. They had weapons in their hands, a machete and a gun to be exact, and they were headed straight towards me. The man with the gun split us up into two groups, pushing my two friends into the sand and pressing the gun into the back of their heads. The second man came up to me, waving his machete and frantically yelling for me to give him my bag and the peridotite gemstone I had around my neck. The two thieves came together and starting talking to each other, seemingly making a new plan.

What was I supposed to do?! Was I going to be kidnapped!? Or worse?? Thoughts starting running through my brain like "grab that jagged rock and hit him over the head if he tries to take you" and "run into the water and try and swim out as far as you can!"

Thankfully they were distracted by a boxer and his trainer who has just appeared on the other side of the beach and they took what they wanted and left, including our rental car keys.

The boxer and his trainer had run out from the road and they told us it was about a 2 mile walk to get help.

My savvy friend disconnected the fuse for the car rental, so the thieves wouldn't be able to start it and we headed on our shaky trek back to the main road. And of course it started to rain. And I slipped in the mud and tore my leg open on a rock. Bleeding, shaking, and completely in shock, we made it to the road where someone took us to the police station.

Our story was a lucky one. Yes we were shaken up but I'm grateful to only have lost property and my pride.

The bandits had made off with everything: our money, our camera with all our photos from the trip, our cell phones, and worst of all, our passports. We had a flight in 48 hours from Managua back to Canada that we didn't want to miss, so we immediately started our emergency passport application to see if we could get it done in time.

Want to know what sped that process up? I had left a photocopy of my credit card, passport, and all other ID with my brother Cody back in Canada. He emailed it over to the Canadian Consulate in Managua so I could prove who I was and get my documents to come back home.

Cody had laughed at me when I gave him all the documents before I left. He was teasing me and making fun of me in typical big brother fashion, telling me I was a worry wart. When I called him, he actually thought it was a joke at first, but then realized I had just escaped a pretty deadly situation.

Another major thing that helped was having good travel insurance. I was able to cover the cost of the emergency passport and my stolen property.

There are a few morals to this story.

1. Have photocopies of your important documents and leave them with someone you are not traveling with. Also keep a copy for yourself securely in the cloud.
2. Do not leave home without travel insurance. EVER!
3. Don't go to secluded beaches, stay for hours, and flash around all your expensive gear. It's not smart.
4. If you find yourself in this awful situation, give them what they want. Your cell phone can be replaced, but your life cannot.
5. Have a loved one know your itinerary, contact information and general whereabouts in case you do go missing.

To be honest, I did suffer post-traumatic stress from this incident for months after returning back to Canada. I was in a movie theatre in the front row and some drunken guy was banging on the exit door from outside behind the building and I lost it! I leapt out of my chair and tried to crawl underneath the row, confusing the people around me. In my head in that moment, it was someone with a gun who was coming to get me, not just a guy banging on a door to be obnoxious.

Being the victim of a violent crime has given me heightened awareness when I travel. I am always looking at my surroundings, judging the body language and tone of peoples' speech, identifying exits and calculating my danger levels. You might say it has instilled some paranoid behaviour into me, but I don't think that it's necessarily a bad thing.

Be safe out there.

On the subject of safety...

Travel Insurance

I use World Nomads for my travel insurance because it allows me to buy as I travel. Many policies need to be setup before leaving the country and that is a buzzkill for my spontaneity.
If I have a sudden change of plans, or I find myself staying longer abroad, I can top it up in minutes online. They have 2 tiers of coverage (one just having more coverage than the other) to pick from, but both are very reasonable considering what they cover.

They are going to cover your butt for things like medical emergencies, stolen property, flight delay, and even trip interruption services.

I also use the travel insurance that comes standard with my credit card. I use the TD Aeroplan Infinite Privilege (which is a super good travel card btw!) and it gives me 22 days of full coverage automatically whenever I leave my home country. So once that runs out, I top it up with World Nomads.

I have said it before and I will say it again. You need travel insurance. Imagine you got into an accident and the bill came out to $350,000? Who has that kind of money sitting around?
Or even on a smaller scale, what if your bag got stolen while you were ordering a cappuccino? It might have had your computer, credit cards, camera and other important gadgets. Are you cool with going to the store and spending thousands of dollars on replacing these items? There are a million different situations I could put into perspective for you, but it all comes down to this:
Get it. Every Time. Without Fail.

25 - Going ALL IN…Without Leaving Home

I get it. The thought of constantly being on flights, in AirBNB's, and train stations might not be your jam. You might have the urge to declutter, downsize, sell most of your crap, pay off all your debt, and still want to stick close to home.
There are still SO many opportunities for you to live a kick ass life that looks very different from the status quo.

RV's & Motorhomes

I had explained in a previous chapter, when Trevor and I live 'at home' in Canada, we live in an RV! We've parked it on a piece of land with a lake view and it will stay there until the end of time. It's small, it's compact, it's cheap, it's perfect. Our bills are microscopic for parked RV insurance and propane fuel, and if we weren't such hopeless wanderlusts, we would probably live in it full time.

I just read an article on a news site about a Canadian man who moved into an RV for 4 years, and was able to pay off almost $100k in debt by doing so! From my own experience in just how cost effective it can be, I absolutely see why more and more people seem to be making the move.
There are thousands of other people who have made the decision to move into a trailer, an RV, a motorhome, or even their vehicle. Some park their home in one spot, and others hit the road with their home on wheels. If your dream is to park an RV somewhere, you need to take into account what the weather is going to be like year round.

Our RV is in the mountains in British Columbia, Canada, meaning there is NO WAY we can live there in the dead of winter. We would go through 1 propane tank a day trying to keep the temperature inside above freezing and our quality of life would suffer. So we take off at the first signs of autumn and don't return until spring has sprung.

I have a girlfriend who travels with her husband in the winter, hooking their RV up to their truck and heading down to the southern states. They seek out cheap RV parks with good Wi-Fi, and escape the harsh Canadian winters in their own mobile estate (seriously, this rig has an island in the kitchen, it's unreal!) With their home rented while they're away, offsetting travel costs becomes super manageable.

No matter if you park it, drive it, or a little bit of both; living in an RV or Motorhome is a perfect way to downsize, save money, and live life on your own terms.

Tiny Homes

I am addicted to watching videos on Tiny Homes! I am always blown away when they tour through how the murphy bed comes down at night, the storage that folds into the wall, or all the ingenious modifications the home goes through to expand and contract as needed. I think the inner child in all of us wants to live in a tiny home. It's like a playhouse for adults!

Aside from all the compelling features, tiny homes are also delightful on the budget.

They need less land to build upon, use less materials, cost less to build, use less labour and time to construct, will cost less to furnish and decorate, and have cheaper utility bills. (Some are even designed to be totally off the grid!)

I don't know how many times I have fantasized about having a quaint tiny home in the countryside, growing my own food in a lush garden and not playing this whole 'let's buy a $750,000 house that I can't afford' game. I bet you have dreamed about it too!

That dream can become a reality. Year after year, trends are showing a huge increase in people giving up the way of life they thought they wanted (cue white picket fence) and making the move into tiny home life.

How much is a tiny home?
They can be built DIY for as low as $6,000, although the average is around $35,000. I've seen some fully built, 400sq ft models that will blow your mind, for around $75,000. No matter how big or small, any tiny home is going to be significantly less than most homes on the market, making them perfect for any high maintenance minimalist.

"Going all in" isn't going to happen on its own. It takes months, if not years, of preparation, research and passion to get rolling. Once you know why you want to live differently, where you want to travel, and how you will support yourself, all the other details can be filled in as you go. Making mistakes is going to happen, and that is perfectly alright! Mistakes are the only way we can learn the difference between the road we don't want to go down, and the perfect path that leads to our destiny.

I am still in awe of how much MORE I can do in this life when I let go. Letting go of the opinions of others, the herd mentality, physical crap taking up space, and panic inducing debts, has allowed me to move into a space of freedom and creativity. Of playfulness and curiosity. Of gratitude and peace.

This is your sign: **Start building the life you want right NOW.**

Part Eight

Families

26 - Doing all of this with KIDS

This topic falls FAR out of my area of expertise. Decluttering, downsizing, paying off debt, becoming an entrepreneur and traveling the world as a woman with NO children is challenging enough, so I can't even begin to imagine what it's like with little ones. When I wrote my first mini book on these subjects, I got hundreds of emails from moms and dads asking for specific help when kids are involved. While I am entirely clueless on all things maternal, I was able to interview some extraordinary families to give us the scoop. I tracked down families who live a minimalist life, teach their kinds about experiences over things, and some who even travel the world together, and asked them to share their best tips and practices for anyone wanting to do the same.

A Different Way Of Life
It doesn't matter if you need advice on how to clear out the family's junk from your house, or if you are looking for guidance on traveling more with your kids, it all comes down to this: A different way of life. You, your spouse and your kids are going to be living life a little differently than the neighbours. While they might be buying even MORE toys to fill the playroom with, you're going to be downsizing the mountainous collection. They might be signing little Susie and Tommy up for summer camp, and you're going to be planning a family excursion in Peru. The first step to improving any aspect of your family's life is knowing you are going to go a little against the grain, and that there is nothing wrong with that.
In business, mentors will commonly tell their eager pupils, "Stay in your lane", meaning, don't worry about what everyone else is doing. Keep your eyes on your goals and pay no attention to what the Jones's are saying. A lot of the pressure, clutter, debt and frustration has been CAUSED by caring too much about what other people think. This is your family and your choice on how you want to live.

The JUNK section

Decluttering and staying organized with kids is no easy feat! I've brought in organized mama **Liz Hawker**, from dreamnourishdiscover.com ,who has great ideas on teaching the art of minimalism to little ones.

"My name is Liz Hawker and I'm currently traveling full time with my husband Scotty and our beautiful 16 month old daughter Sienna Bella. I have a passion for natural living, gentle parenting and minimalism.

In December 2016 we took a huge leap of faith.
Our daughter was 4.5 months old and we packed up our house, selling or giving away the majority of our belongings and set off on a world trip with no end date in sight. We didn't want to spend our lives wondering 'what if' and we knew that if things didn't work out we could always book a flight 'home'. There is so much beauty in the world and I love being able to share it with our daughter and see it through her eyes as she experiences everything for the first time.
My husband is a professional ultra marathon runner and online running coach. We are currently following Scotty's race calendar around the world with a few side trips included for relaxation and time with our beautiful family. Sienna Bella and I spend our days hiking, swimming and playing at the park while Scotty works and trains. At night I plan wellness events, training camps for Scotty, and of course, our next adventure!"

Liz's tips and ideas to assist you in living a more minimalist lifestyle with your family:

1. One of the most important things to remember is: ***it doesn't have to be all or nothing.*** Start with making small changes that you're comfortable with, but also keep in mind that being a little bold and courageous could lead to something amazing.
Downsizing and decluttering can be extremely therapeutic. Speak to family and friends to see if they'd like to join you in moving towards a more minimalist lifestyle.

2. Something my husband and I live by, and would like to pass on to our daughter, is **the value of 'experiences over things'**. Creating memories is far more rewarding and something you can hold on to for a lifetime, as opposed to material items that usually bring short-lived enjoyment and quite often end up gathering dust.

3. There are so many free or cheap 'experiences' that you can share with your children. Sienna Bella and I love hiking and we use this as a way to explore new places that we visit. We also enjoy going to local swimming pools, or to the beach if we're close to the coast. Something as simple as finding new parks to play at can be such a fun way to spend time with your children.

4. We have very few toys for our daughter, and instead prefer to spend our time in nature where she can use her imagination to entertain herself. She loves playing with rocks and sticks, and finding flowers in the grass. If your children are a bit older, a 'scavenger hunt' could be a fun activity for them. You can draw (or get them to draw) a list of items (a feather, rock, shell etc) and head outside to see what you can find. **Children have the most amazing imaginations** and it's so important to nurture their ever-expanding minds as they grow up.

5. If you have too many toys and you're wondering how to downsize, you can start by sorting through them all. Put everything that you don't think your children play with often into a box (depending on their age this is something they could help you with).
If they don't ask for the toys that are in the box for two weeks you can then look to selling them or donating them to charity. This is a good way of doing a large cull all at once.

6. A great rule to use when purchasing any new items/toys/clothing is **'One In, Two Out'** which means that for each new item you bring into the home, you must sell or give away two items you already have. If this feels like too much, you can start with 'One In, One Out' and progress from there.

7. For our daughter's 1st birthday we asked close friends and family to contribute to a time capsule that we will give Sienna Bella when she turns 18. Not only does it mean that she wasn't gifted lots of presents that she might not use (and that we don't have luggage space for) but it will be a beautiful keepsake for her to treasure once she's older. This idea could be used for any birthday or special occasion.

I've asked another minimalist mama to chime in with her top tips as well. **Clarissa Yates**, the creator of hookedinabox.com talks about her own struggle with consumerism and what has worked for her family.

"My name is Clarissa and I am a mum to two young girls, Elsie (2) and Madeleine (6 months). Before I moved to Australia, I lived in Singapore my whole life. The culture in Singapore is very much about 'buy first, think later'. There were ads plastered everywhere and you could try easily be sucked into a consumeristic mentality while there. There's a huge focus on brands and being known as somebody, thus a lot of Singaporeans buy a lot of things they cannot afford to 'live up to the look'. I too fell into that trap and was spending my entire month's salary on items I didn't need, clothes, shoes, bags, anything to make me feel good. Then I moved to Perth, and I could not afford to spend the way I did, as I was a fresh international student living a pauper life. I learned so much about saving and buying only what I needed and my experience living as an international student in a foreign country taught me a lot about being minimalistic.
Fast-track to 2015 when I gave birth to my first child. Being an overly excited first-time mum, I bought all the 'things' I thought I needed for her. In hindsight almost everything I bought other than the major important items was wasted. When I gave birth to my second, that's when I really put my foot down about buying more things. We also had built our first house, and that gave me an opportunity to donate/clean/throw away as many items as possible so that we didn't bring all my junk with me. In the end, when we moved, I was so shocked and embarrassed at how much stuff I had! We filled out an entire truck and most of the items were mine! I did not want to bring my girls up this way. Thus, I became a minimalistic mum and my kids and I are so much happier because of it!"

Clarissa's top tips for being a minimalistic mum:

- **Resist the urge** to buy them cheap, plastic toys that just create more waste and takes up space in your house.
- Wait till a special event: birthday/Christmas to buy them something. The most number of presents you buy for them is 2 not 20 small ones.
- When you buy something for them, ask yourself if your child will get a lot of use out of this, is this a nice thing to donate once your child is done with it? **If the answer is no, don't get it.**
- Clean out your child's toys/clothes/items every 6 months or so and donate or store away for next child.
- When you are done with children, donate ALL toys away.
- Never give in to a child that wants you to get that one item from the shop, it may seem mean but it's better to let your child wait for special events to get gifts, and that makes it all the more special.
- My simple rule for cleaning out: *if it hasn't been touched, used, seen for the last year, chuck it out.*
- Store your kid's items in large transparent containers, because if you hide the toys in spots you can't see, you end up just dumping items everywhere - out of sight, out of mind.
- Allow your child to be bored, teach them to be bored. They learn how to be imaginative and creative with what they have.
- Always pick natural or use existing items you have for children to play with. You will be surprised how fun your normal household items are to them.
- **Teach your children the value of money;** that things cost money and some things are not needed. Always go with less is more.

The MONEY Section

Money and the concept of budgeting can be confusing for children to understand. For this topic, I've got financial educator and money mentor **Michelle House** from michellehouse.com.au giving her insider secrets.

I've been through a recession with my first business at the age of 22, a global financial crisis AND we even have been faced with $75,000 in consumer debt, tinkering on the edge of bankruptcy.
It wasn't easy.
There was the messy breakdown on the kitchen floor which included the ugly cry and lots of snot, the sleepless nights because my heart would beat so loud I couldn't sleep and then there was that tense feeling between me and my husband as we worried our way through the days.
And then there was the surrender. The "I'm doing everything I can with everything I know - please help me" moment.

I started taking action. Taking small steps and kept moving forward and everything turned around.
Now, I teach others exactly how to get everything they've ever wanted in life. The money and the life. Because you can't have one without the other.

RICH is ...
- Reflection
- Inspiration
- Conscious
- Harmony

Reflection - Journal your Spending

I've been in this money space for many years now. As a single lady, a newlywed, as a mum and household finance manager and this has to be my top must do tip. If you only do one thing, do this:
Track your spending for 30 days.

Here's what I know for sure. Money isn't just about the numbers. Our financial position is about our behaviour. It's how we feel about it. When we are busy with kids and just getting through the day our behaviour with money changes.

Let me be really clear. This exercise isn't about beating yourself with a stick. It's an awareness exercise, because when we become aware of something, that's when we have a choice to make - to change or not to change.

Track your spending for a good 30 days and write down everything you are spending your money on. Coins from the car, paypass and any late night eBay purchases online - write them down. This tracking is for what I call variable spending. It varies day to day based on our behaviour (how annoying the kids are being, how much sleep we've had, if the mother in law is coming round - #youknowwhatimean).

After 30 days go through and highlight everything that was a NEED (groceries, new undies, nappies etc.) and with a different colour highlight all the WANTS.

When you can see what you are doing with your money, your *aha's* will pop in. Oh look at that ... I didn't do any meal planning that week and our groceries doubled. Oops ... did I spend that much on bottled water?

PS... **this is a great activity to get the kids involved with.** The more they see you respecting your money, the more they learn. It is SOOOOO important that kids understand early about money. What things cost, what' reasonable, what is value etc.

Inspiration - Teaching kids about money

Teaching kids about debt and overspending is a lesson in behaviour!! The way we talk about money will create their doubts, their limiting beliefs so it's important that we think about what we say.

For example: telling our kids constantly that we can't afford it is going to create that belief for them in their own life. It might be true, that you can't afford it. But re-wording it into something like: HOW can we afford it? Approaching from a curious place and getting them thinking about HOW.

Let's say they really want a new bike and you really want them to have one. Instead of **I can't afford it**, embrace curiosity and question how can we afford a new bike. Maybe it's selling the old bike, or having a garage sale or entering a competition for a new bike.

If you have credit card debt, show them. Show them how it works, how you bought something for half price and now you are paying interest on it.

Conscious Spending

I have to use that word because I reckon we've all become pay pass zombies - tapping here for a coffee, tapping there for some lego, tapping over here for some new sports shoes.
We have to wake up and get purposeful about our spending.
And teach the kids while we are at it.
Take a moment to think before you whack another purchase on your card.
Could I get this online for free? Is there a better alternative?
Is this an impulse buy?

Harmony

Here's the aim. Harmony. Getting to the place where you feel confident, clear and calm about the ebbs and flow of money in your life. Just like the stock market, property and life, you will have ups and downs with your financial situation. Things happen that are beyond our control - tech bubbles burst, global financial crisis, recessions and being prepared for those help you go through them with ease and grace.

The TRAVEL Section

In doing research for this chapter, I ran into a ton of globetrotting families who have a lot of experience traveling with little ones. I asked them to spill the beans on their best travel tips and advice to share with you.

Top 10 Tips for Traveling with Kids (as told by traveling parents):

- If you and your partner are separated, you will need written permission to leave the country with your children.

- Most airlines let children 2 and under (who are on a parents lap) fly for free. A lot of families take advantage of this before those tickets become full fare.

- Pack light, plan ahead. Many popular tourist destinations will have things like car seats, cribs, playpens, strollers and other necessities easily available for rent. If the thought of dragging strollers through the airport is enough to keep you staying at home, plan to have it available at your destination instead.

- Load up on entertainment. Delays happen, but what makes them much easier to deal with is having entertained kids. Load the iPad up with movies, games, books, and other distractions to minimize the stress of an already long travel day.

- Pull them out of school. Chill, it's just for a few days! No child will ever tell you later in life "mom, that time you pulled me out of second grade a few days before Christmas was a big mistake. I missed important schoolwork, like never learning how to properly draw a Santa hat!" They don't mind and a few days here and there aren't going to disrupt their education. When you only travel on major holidays, the flights, accommodation and everything in between is highly marked up. Leaving just a few days earlier can make a huge difference in the cost of your family vacation!

- Ask for a mini fridge to be put in your hotel room, or ask the existing one be emptied of expensive juice/booze. This way you can fill it with healthy (and cheaper) snacks and have more freedom in between meals.

- Kid and Coe is a vacation rental site just like Airbnb or Homeaway that specializes in kid friendly vacations. All homes are kid safety approved, toys and strollers are waiting for you upon arrival and locations have family focused attractions.

- Give them a camera. Having your kids operate a camera will keep them busy, dialed into their surroundings, and will get the creative juices flowing. They will take more time to look at the details and beauty around them, plus they will create some fantastic shots for the scrapbook.

- Have kids carry their own backpacks to help lighten the load. Parents will inevitably be pushing everyone's luggage through the airport, so make packing backpacks with essentials a fun game. Your kids will be more aware of what they have in their sacks and take pride in the independence.

- Your kids deserve to see the world. Make it a priority over toys, dining out, and other budget busters.

27 - Families Who Are Doing It!

I love hearing from people who have 'been there, done that', as I find it so inspirational and real! I interviewed 2 families for this book, to give you a window into their mindsets about education, minimalism and travel. They are living examples of how ANYONE can decide to live a more minimalistic or nomadic life, regardless of what their family might look like.

Meet the 1st Family: The Swindlers

"I'm Shannan Swindler. My travel motto is "Have Passport; Will Travel". I can pack a travel itinerary the same way I pack my carry-on. Tight, exciting, and on budget.
My first trip to Europe was in 1995. I thought it was going to be one of those "once-in-a-lifetime" adventures. Little did I know that I was just re-orienting my compass and charting a whole new course with dreams of living overseas someday.
Between 2008 and 2015, that dream was nearly snuffed out and forgotten. After a series of life-changing events, we re-kindled the dream to raise our family overseas. With renewed direction, passion and a "no regrets" lifestyle, we packed up our family in 8 suitcases and 8 carry-ons and moved to Scotland. People thought we were crazy. We are. We're that kind of crazy that makes you want to live life to the fullest.
Now, we travel, and homeschool, from our home base in Scotland. When the itch to travel needs a good scratch (like every 6 weeks or so), we grab our passports and find the cheapest flight to anywhere. Literally. It's kinda like playing spin the bottle with your passport. You never know who you might end up with!

I blog about our ambitious adventures at captivatingcompass.com as we travel with kids while being homeschooling expats. We try to travel on a budget and see the best of the best whilst leaving something in the bank for the next adventure."

Shannan, why did you decide to go the homeschooling route?

Back in 2012, with a six-year-old and a toddler, I never dreamed of homeschooling. We loved our neighbourhood school & everyone associated with it. However, my kids both became ill. My 6 year-old had to withdraw from school in order to recover from her illness and a surgery. We participated in an online charter school for the remainder of the year to keep up. We honestly figured we would start again at the brick and mortar school the next fall. Over the summer, someone told me about co-ops. I fell in love with the ideas of community days and independent family learning. Homeschooling became our new normal.

What problems do you see with the traditional way of life for a family?

If by "traditional" you mean "the American dream", I think the problem is that it's not really achievable any more. It was for our parents, for the most part. But now higher education is extortionate (compared to other countries) and the need for it to achieve the "job of your dreams" has produced many who have amassed an incredible amount of knowledge and degrees, but lack the people skills and experience to make it in the real world. Technology has changed us in this regard and allowed us to become more flexible with our time, talents and location.

Have you ever thought about becoming fully nomadic with your family?

Yes! I'm dying to, and we will get there. Currently we are in a bit of transition. We knew from the beginning Scotland was a stepping stone, but we were not sure what was next.

How has 'world schooling' changed the attitudes/outlook in your kids?

They are certainly more flexible in their thinking and more tolerant in their ideas about others.

They recognize the importance of thinking globally and how difficult that is. We are trying to instill in them that people and experiences are more important than things. The experiences shape our worldview and stretch us. The interaction with a variety of people helps them understand the beauty of other cultures and ways of doing things.

Would you call yourselves minimalists?

Well, possibly. We moved to Scotland with only 8 suitcases and 8 carry-ons. We sold most everything else and only have a few things in storage until we decide what is best to do with some keepsakes. While we have begun to accumulate a few things and it is time for a clear out, I would view us as budding minimalists.

It is a process. We realize after every trip away, we don't need as many of the things that seem so important to us. If we have each other, food and a roof over our heads we've got more than most and are grateful.

What have you had to sacrifice in order to live this way?

We struggle to maintain strong relationships with friends and family back home. But, that is a two way street, so I won't blame it all on us. We have however been set free to pursue our passions and dreams without living under as many "shoulds" imposed by those close to us.

What about the HARD parts?

The hardest part for us was doing what we knew was right for our family in spite of other family members not being thrilled with us. Those were tethers that were holding us back from our potential. Of course we miss our family and need to work hard at honouring them and maintaining relationships with them. The key is finding the balance and creating understanding and a sense of belonging for everyone involved - no matter the distance.

What is the BEST thing about your way of life?

We are seeing the world, creating really tight sibling and nucleus family bonds.
We have been able to host others to allow them to see parts of the world they would not be able to afford without a place to call home for a few days. We have made friends with folks from all over Europe and the world.

What would you say to moms/dads that feel they CAN'T do something like this?
Come join the fun! You might be thinking that you can't do this. But I believe you can.
It's about looking out your front window at what is in your world and setting out for an adventure to understand it at a deeper level than you did the day before. No matter where you live. With technology and a spirit of adventure, every family that desires to can be a world schooling/minimalistic family!

Next we have our 2nd fully nomadic family: The Pamley-Liddell's

This British family of five fell into nomadism through desperation but loved it so much they couldn't stop traveling.
Their family consists of two parents and three kids, ranging from seven to fourteen years in age. They took on the world after leaving the UK in 2011 in search of a better work-life balance.
After four years in luscious Australia, their visa wasn't renewed and they returned to mainland Europe in search of different delights. The static life wasn't for them so they sold their furniture, left only their most precious possessions in storage and set off with too many bags *(ha!)* to discover what the world had to offer. They blog about their adventures at journeyofanomadicfamily.com

I talked to Emma about what it's like to be a fully nomadic family on the road:

How long have you been nomadic?

We started out being location independent in March 2016 but being based in France. We became nomadic in November 2016.

What prompted you to change your way of life? Was it a turning point moment, something said, or a realization?

We were born and raised in the UK (England) but we were frustrated with our lives.
We were working LONG hours and for not really much reward. 7/8ths of my salary was spent on childcare and a big proportion to mortgage. We managed to get ourselves into debt and the future looked bleak and unappealing.

Richard was approached about a job in Australia and as we had nothing to lose we left in 2011. After four brilliant years in Perth & Brisbane our visa was not renewed and we had no option but to leave for France. I have a degree in French (as well as social work) so we thought it would be a pretty easy transition but it turned out to be the wrong move for us. We became location independent in a bid to save money to escape France but then we really enjoyed it and decided to carry on traveling.

How do you know homeschooling and 'world-schooling' is going to give your children a proper education?

So many people leave school unable to read, write or arithmitise. They lack the skills that are required to get fulfilling jobs and more often than not they lack confidence. If school cannot prepare children with an education for later life, can we really do as bad a job?
We give our children an eclectic range of learning materials which encourages them to adapt to new ways of learning and thinking. I think they're much more resourceful now than when they were at school. In many ways school is no longer about education, it's about reproducing facts for tests. This doesn't inspire them to love learning.

The more we travel the more we use wildschooling and unschooling. Two techniques that require the child to drive his learning ambitions. It is proving very successful.

What about their friends?

This is an area that challenges us.
Our children make friends wherever they go but they also have static friends they can go back to. They miss these friends but they don't take them for granted.

Isn't it dangerous!?

Define danger. Crossing the road can be dangerous but we wouldn't avoid doing that.
I don't think traveling is dangerous but then I don't define risk as negative. I see risk as a positive aspect; we learn and grow from taking risks and it makes us much more resilient to change. I would be bored shitless if I never took risks.

What if they get sick?

Exposing your children to a wide variety of germs protects and strengthens their immune system. In the last 18 months they've been sick once. We're intelligent, educated, level-headed people. We also have a first aid course. If your child gets sick you keep an eye on them; replenish their fluids and make sure they don't deteriorate.

Every country I've been to has had local pharmacies which stock medicines. They're often MUCH cheaper than our own countries and you can buy all sorts of prescription medicine over the counter.
We do have medical insurance which covers us for emergencies. We've never used it and don't intend to.

Don't kids need stability to develop?

It would appear not! As a democratic family we listen to our kids. They love to explore and have adventures but equally they enjoy down time when they can play lego, play-doh & Roblox.
We recently spent 11 weeks fast traveling 6 countries in SE Asia. They had an amazing time and of course they had no access to toys, as we only had 2 backpacks, but then they had enough.
We're now having some down time in rural Bulgaria (which is frustrating for me who wants to explore) and I have to respect their needs at this time.

As a family we're already planning a trip to Iceland and Mexico and they're really excited about that. They google things to do and places to stay and look at images. They're fascinated by nature and the world needs more environmentalists so let's nurture that.

How do you earn $$ traveling?

We run our own businesses; Rich is a consulting engineer and I am a photographer.

What is the hardest thing about this lifestyle?

I am very happy now (think 9/10) but I really miss my computer which is in our storage unit. It's such a silly thing but it was custom designed for me and it's a joy to work on. It makes processing photos very quick and easy.

What is the BEST thing about this lifestyle?

Only one thing? Meeting new people. I have met some truly inspiring people along this path and I hope to meet many more.

What SACRIFICES have you made in order to live like this?

We have no house, no car, no credit history and we live very frugally out of backpacks. I am a vegan foodie and I do miss my blenders and my cookery equipment. I have grown to like my kindle book reader but nothing can beat the smell of a book.

What changes have you noticed in your kids (before vs now)?

Good question! Some changes have been developmentally in line with their age but others have been more apparent.

Their confidence is much greater. Their ability to read situations is developing quite well. They pick up languages relatively easily and aren't afraid to have a go. They play with other kids despite the language barrier and have developed some sort of strange sign language to communicate. Ability to read timetables and train stations and where we should get on/off is brilliant. Geography is hugely improving.

Their reading and comprehension is very accomplished because we spend time reading blurbs at tourist sites etc.

My eldest is already a qualified diver and is happy to go off diving alone with a group etc and not with us. The younger two snorkel fantastically and have started free diving.

Problem solving is really a noticeable skill in my 14 year old. I messed up and got us to the airport in Belgrade a day late (stupid 2am mistake) which meant that our flight to Athens had left and there weren't any more. There was a flight to Thessaloniki which we grabbed and boarded within 20 minutes. As we were all looking for solutions on how to get to Athens at 3am, it was my daughter who found us a train. Her entrepreneurial skills are also developing and she would love to make more money online. She has sold some designs.

What would you say to people that claim "I can't just go traveling the world! I have KIDS and that kind of life is just a pipe dream!"?

If you want it to happen, you'll make it happen. You have to be of the right mindset to even consider having this lifestyle.

These are some powerful and inspiring families, right?
One thing I see in common between all of them has been their ability to take action towards a dream they desperately wanted to manifest.
I hope they have motivated you to do the same!
No matter what your goals are, get your spouse involved, get your kids involved and take one small step towards your dream life!

Part Nine

FREEDOM

Freedom. It's the word that has been my driving force this entire time. Freedom from the outdated template of life, freedom from the crippling opinions of others, freedom from monotony, freedom from debt and consumerism.
The freedom to blaze my own trail.
But even freedom comes with a cost.

Sacrifices

The question I get asked the most is: "How can you afford to travel all the time!?"

Let me be the first one to tell you, it has nothing to do with the amount I make. People successfully travel the world on less than $15,000 a year, while others need at least $200,000. It comes down to my lifestyle, my resourcefulness and my creativity.
When I hear people say they could NEVER afford to travel all the time, in most cases, I know it's not true. What they are saying is "There are other things in my life that are more important to me, and therefore what I spend my money on instead of traveling."

If you want to travel more, then do it.
Find the sacrifice.

My sacrifice was a house, a car, and 95% of my clothing and shoes. If I had kept those things, at this time in my life, there would be no way I could travel full time without going into debt.
Traveling, seeing the world, and designing my own life is SO much more important than doing the good ol' 'mortgage game' along with many of my peers.

As my business grows, and my income grows, the WAY I travel will likely change. For now it's a mix between short luxury stops and long term affordable stays. I ebb and flow.
I might spend 3 nights at a 5 star hotel, following with a month at a local AirBNB apartment.

I do what I can, with what I have. I don't press the limits. If I can stay out of debt, still have money to contribute to savings and retirement, and I'm being realistic... then I go for it!

If I can't afford it without a payment plan, then I go without until I'm able.

Tonight we are taking the Night Riviera Sleeper train from London to Penzance. It will be my first time in a sleeper train! How cool right?! Your own bedroom on a train where you wake up to breakfast in bed as the sun comes up over the coast of England.

I've always wanted to do this!

When I first started looking at sleeper trains, my eyes almost fell out of my head. A cross country VIA Rail sleeper in Canada can cost upwards of $12,000. Luxury trains traveling through Siberia or Africa can charge between $20k-$40k.

But, through hours of Googling and a willingness to sacrifice with what I have to work with at this moment, I found a way to still have an experience for less.

I bought 2 tickets from GWR for $140 Canadian dollars for this ride. It gives us 2 hours in the first class lounge before departure sipping on champagne, a private room with beds on the train, access to the Pullman dining car for onboard drinks and snacks, and breakfast in bed at the end of the 9 hour journey. WINNING!

Is it as fancy as the luxury Russian trains? Nope! But that's not the point. The point is, by being open, resourceful and creative; I'm able to travel in new and exciting ways. By applying that same level of resourcefulness to other areas in my life, I get the same kind of wonderful results.

What sacrifices will you make in your life to get what you want?

What scares me?

As I finish this book, I'm sitting in a London train station, reading the local news paper.

The front page headline reads "Millions of Britons Face Pension Poverty" with the very first sentence reaffirming the scary details.

"Britain is on the brink of a crisis in personal finance, with figures showing that more than four million people have repeatedly failed to pay their bills in the past six months"
And
"Half of the adult population, more than 25 million people, has been identified as potentially vulnerable to financial harm."

I see the same headlines referring to Canadians when in Canada, and Americans when in the United States.
It seems this issue isn't regional, it's spreading globally.

The facts about personal finance in the UK are this: 1/4 of the population has gone into overdraft in the past year, 25% of Brit's have less than $1000 in savings, and almost 1/3 of the country hovering the poverty line and simply 'surviving' on their wages.
There is talk about rising bank rates and the fear of how it will send many families spiraling into more debt and despair.

The article then goes on to talk about how the average person can avoid this kind of financial demise. "Build up a cash savings, increase your pension payments, pay off your debt in your twenties"
……*For real?*

These tips are too little too late.
Half of the adult population doesn't have the funds to save extra money, pay off debt faster, or contribute more to their retirement. This advice is like selling a starving man a cookbook, he can't get what he really needs by simply reading the words on the pages.

What I do NOT see in this article, or any other news story like it, is the discussion of WHY this is truly happening. At best, I'll find some vague stats on how wages are at an all time low and cost of living is at an all time high. Sure. That is obvious.
Let's talk about the not so obvious reasons why people default on their mortgage or can't pay their bills.

SPENDING

People are spending money that should be going towards basic needs (like housing, food and healthcare) on iPhones, Ubers and Redbull instead.

I don't blame them, in fact I find myself frequently doing the very same thing, but it's a massive issue that needs to be addressed.
But it won't. Because the big consumerism machine needs to be fuelled by peoples wages to keep trucking along. If we started talking about the irreversible damage we are doing on our own financial wellbeing, that wouldn't be good news for them.

I'm people watching in Paddington Station at this very moment.
I'm looking at the average everyday commuter, Starbucks in one hand and smart phone in the other. This is also the same person who might be short on his rent next month and resort to borrowing money at 29% from some 'Quick Cash' market down the street, only adding to his financial burden.
Does he know that without all his latest gadgets, daily brand name coffee habits and weekly H&M stops, that he could afford his rent? Or that it would allow him to afford healthy meals, the roof over his head, and perhaps to even contribute to his future? He likely does know that somewhere deep down, but he chooses the life of distraction and short term gratification. He lives in denial that he will be part of the 25% of Briton's that fall into default, so he continues to press the limits on his life style.

We took a walking tour through a once derelict, but now hipster hot district in London. On the outskirts of this cultural melting pot neighbourhood, the city streets still found themselves in disarray. From the sidewalk in front of the dilapidated apartment buildings, I could see inside many of the resident's living rooms. Flat screens, Xboxes, plastic containers from last night's Chinese takeout, and a pre-teen girl playing a game on a smart phone. I'm not saying this family doesn't deserve these things, I believe everyone deserves modern technology and fun distractions in life, but what if these items are keeping them below the poverty line? What if these consumerism habits are adding up to hundreds or even thousands a month, keeping them unable to pay for education, proper health care, or retirement?
That would be a fucking shame.

Yes, wages need to be higher. Yes, the cost of living needs to come into a reasonable realm. And YES, the conversation of consumerism and the financial pain it can cause needs to happen.

Living in this neon society is expensive. And if you don't keep up with everyone else, you are shunned from the herd. It's tough. It's not easy. It's much easier to go out for wings and a pint with friends, spending the last $15 in your account, instead of paying off your credit card. However, that will only be 'easier' until the credit runs out, then reality hits you like a freight train.

I just experienced how fast it can get out of hand over the last week. Since Trevor and I spend the majority of our life traveling, we have to get super creative with not spending tons of cash, to keep ourselves out of debt.
Last week I was invited to take a 72 hour tour of London by the local board, and then we had 4 days of a hectic pre-launch of Trevor's UK business, finishing with a weekend of events and conferences. We got busy! And because of that, we got sloppy.
Our Oyster cards (for the London Underground Subway) ran out of money, and instead of just reloading them at the station, we starting taking Uber's. We were running around 16 hours of the day and being too tired to grocery shop and make cheap healthy meals in our hotel suite, we ordered some room service. Instead of filling up our water bottles with the free filtration system in the lobby, we bought new ones at the corner store. I said "YOLO" and ordered that $28 glass of wine from the bar beside the hotel instead of walking 2 minutes down the road to an affordable pub.
All of these mistakes added UP!
I checked my credit card statement today and there was about 380 British Pounds (Or about $620 Canadian dollars) of money I had not budgeted for, from only a week of being indulgent.
Add that up over 52 weeks and that would equal over $32,000. I don't know about you guys but that makes me feel faint! $32k is considered someone's healthy WAGE, not a 'whoopsie' budget. These additional purchases all started with me saying "Oh it's only like $8 more than making food" or "The Uber is $3 more but gets us there faster, it's all good" I meant well, but I was screwing myself over.

This makes me wonder how many other people are literally screwing themselves into debt. Letting those tiny little innocent "It's only $2!" add up over days, months and weeks, until they are drowning in payments.

Convenience, comparison and consumerism is making us broke.

How can we complain about wages and inflation when we can't be trusted with our own spending habits?
Being underpaid and living in a world that costs too much is creating debt, but equally so, is our desire to have MORE.
I'm not talking about the single mother who walks to work, takes on double shifts, and spends every spare cent she has on food and shelter. I'm talking about the average Jane who is naively hugging the poverty line, whose debt grows each month, but it doesn't stop her from buying two bottles of wine each week or spending half her pay check on luxury high heels.

Why are we not taught how to avoid the pitfall of this lifestyle? There isn't a class in school that teaches pupils about responsible consumerism, comparison and instant gratification. Actually, the only guidance we get on these subjects is from advertisers, corporations, banks and big business, and they all tell us to keep pushing the limits. The only education I have ever received on this topic was a week in elementary where we briefly covered things like mortgages, savings accounts and retirement. Never anything about a drone based lifestyle that is hurting us mentally and emotionally, and that is a pity.

While I am just one person, my wish is that bringing light to these topics will give more power and hope to the people who want to live a better life.

What Gives me HOPE

It was only a few years ago when I found myself at rock bottom. I believe it was, cliche enough, in a bathroom stall, curled up in the corner wondering how I gotten myself into such a mess. The pressure was too much and I was trying to numb it with booze, drugs, flirtations and mindless spending, but it just kept getting worse. I started making massive mistakes and abusing the trust of those closest to me, in a full fledged self sabotaging train to nowhere. I fucked up. Big time.

That night in the bathroom stall, shaking and scared, I made a promise to the powers that be. If they could help me get out of this wreck, I would change my ways forever.

The next day I pulled the plug. I literally hit the 'reset' button on my entire life, the same way you would reset a desktop computer. Somewhere in the midst of all the chaos, I started to understand where I had gone wrong, and I started to feel hopeful about my future again. Not knowing what to do, or how to do it, I just went forward anyway, remembering the promise I had made. As luck or divinity would have it, here I am, living a life that is free of all the pressures that had once driven me into madness.

My life isn't perfect, but it's finally a life I am excited to show up in every day.

Once I started sharing all the life changes I was going through on social media, my inbox filled with more messages than I had ever seen before. People were telling me they felt exactly the same way I did, or that they were currently dealing with more debt or pressure than they could bare. It made me realize my past was not an anomaly or exception to the rule, but that what had plagued me was also tormenting others. Immediately I began to see my purpose.

I am eternally grateful that I have the opportunity to help others through my own experiences. To have a stage and voice to inspire others is something I never take for granted.

This book was born out of a burning desire to try and help as many people as I possibly can, because I know what it's like to feel crippled by the pressure of society.

What gives me hope is watching the excitement and the energy that is released from people who start making positive changes in their life. A few months ago I wrote a mini-book on the same topics that are covered in these pages, and the feedback I started getting was extraordinary. People were writing in to me telling me that once they put a few of my tips into play, they were saving $50, $200, $500, even $1000 a month!

Other emails talked about how my book came to them at the exact time they needed it most, right before they gave up on their dreams, which they are now working harder than ever towards.

I got pictures of newly cleaned up houses with smiling people who said they have never felt freer, and messages about debts being paid off in record time. People told me their travel goals, bucket lists and wanderlust dreams. They confessed to me what they've always wanted to do for a living, with plans to break free from monotony and finally take a chance on themselves.

I saw hundreds of people starting to change their lives for the better, and it flooded my heart with more love than I can explain.

I never imagined that my own journey into happiness would spread into the lives of others.

Open dialogue, a sense of community and collaboration is how we will change our own lives, and the world, for the better.

So what's next?

For me, I am going to keep pushing forward into my life as a high maintenance minimalist, traveling the world with my husband, and showing others the magic of living with less. I'm going to dive further into making more lifestyle hacks. I'm going to chat with other experts and interview them on my upcoming podcast. I'm going to share more of my day to day life as a full time travel girl. Each new place I visit and each day that passes on the road, I am learning more and more about myself and creating a life by design. I'll never stop sharing that with others in hopes I can make a positive impact in their future. In YOUR future.

What's next for you? Right now, **anything you want.**

Every new day is a blank canvas that you can paint the way you want it to be. You don't have to live life the same way as your parents, your neighbours, or your friends. The stock market and the banks don't have to dictate where and how you live. You don't need to own a bunch of personal items to be worthy of love. You don't have to live inside the box you've been stuffed into along the way.

I hope you take action on each step of this book, making your life richer in every aspect of the word.

You are the master of your universe and powerful enough to create your deepest desires, all you need is to take the first step. Nothing is out of reach and nothing is impossible.

Like Toni Morrison once said; "Can't nobody fly with all that shit. Wanna fly, you got to give up the shit that weighs you down."
Listen to your heart, shake off all the weight, and just GO for it!

My dream is that your debt gets erased, your life becomes organized, as you step into your dream career, and start experiencing more than you ever thought possible.
'Things' will come and go, but the memories we make are the true measure of a good life.

Freedom. *What will yours look like?*

Acknowledgements

They say it takes a village to raise a child, well I think it takes one to write a book as well! There are many people who selflessly devoted their time, advice and information that was vital to making this book a reality.

A huge thanks to my husband Trevor, who fed me and reminded me to shower while I was lost in the vortex of writing. Victoria Kenzington, thank you for lending your creative style and putting up with seven hundred text messages from me per day. Also for being the best photographer and cover art designer a girl could ever ask for. Helen Munroe, you have the patience of a saint for editing my book and fixing the never ending spelling and grammar mistakes. Who would have thought I ever passed English class? This book would not exist without your help. My parents, Tripp & Lynda Parmiter, thanks for teaching me to always go against the grain and hustle for what I want. You wandering gypsies really rubbed off on me, and I couldn't be happier about that. Natalie (Diver) Ellis, thank you for being an inspiring mentor and getting me out of my shell. Your advice has been a huge kick in my ass to make dreams a reality much sooner than I thought possible.

A huge thank you to my experts who gave great advice on the family chapter; Clarissa Yates, Michelle House, Liz Hawker, Emma Pamley-Liddell, & Shannan Swindler.

To my dear friends who let me talk their ear off and ask book related questions to: Lauren Steele, Julie Stewart-Binks, Krystal Fournier, Stacy & Mats Lundgren, Marilyn & Wayne Kucheran.

And finally, to my rock bottom, for giving me the motivation to finally change.

To the Reader: *I wrote this book for YOU.*
I would love to hear how it's made a positive impact in your life. Connect with me personally at:
hello@thehighmaintenanceminimalist.com
Send me your stories, questions, comments, or just to say HI!

Resources & Extras

Since you are either reading this book in paperback, or on an eReader, I created some extra resources for you online

Exclusive Deals & Discounts For My Readers:
Traveloffpath.com/deals

Hotel & Airline Loyalty & Points Programs:
Traveloffpath.com/points

Printable & Editable Workbooks:
Traveloffpath.com/workbooks

About The Author

Kashlee Kucheran is a well known lifestyle and business mentor, who has inspired many to create their own life of freedom and abundance. She traded her real estate and finance careers to travel the world full time with her husband Trevor. When she isn't on a plane or in a hotel, she's based out of Kelowna, BC Canada.

Connect with her on Social Media:

Kashlee's Instagram:
@kashlee_k

Travel Off Path Instagram:
@traveloffpath

Luxury Travel Tour Instagram:
@luxurytraveltour

Facebook Page:
www.facebook.com/trevorandkashlee

Blog:
www.traveloffpath.com

Made in the USA
San Bernardino, CA
29 November 2018